Changing Urban Education

Resources to accompany this book are available online at: http://education.prattadams.continuumbooks.com

Please visit the link and register with us to receive your password and to access these downloadable resources.

If you experience any problems accessing the resources, please contact Continuum at: info@continuumbooks.com

Also available from Continuum

Comparative and International Education, David Phillips, Michele Schweisfurth and Erwin Epstein

International Perspectives on Education, Chau Meng Huat and Trevor Kerry

Changing Urban Education

Simon Pratt-Adams, Meg Maguire and Elizabeth Burn

Contemporary Issues in Education Studies

continuum

Continuum International Publishing Group
The Tower Building   80 Maiden Lane
11 York Road   Suite 704
London SE1 7NX   New York, NY 10038

www.continuumbooks.com

British Library Cataloguing-in-Publication Data
A catalogue record for this book is available from the British Library.

ISBN: 9781847060242 (paperback)
        9781441170705 (hardcover)

Library of Congress Cataloging-in-Publication Data
A catalog record for this book is available from the Library of Congress.

Typeset by Newgen Imaging Systems Pvt Ltd, Chennai
Printed and bound in Great Britain by CPI Antony Rowe Ltd,
   Chippenham, Wiltshire

Contents

Series Editors' Preface

The series Contemporary Issues in Education Studies is timely for its critical exploration of education in this period of accelerating change. Responding to this challenge, the books in the series have titles which correspond closely to the needs of students taking a wide range of courses and modules within Education Studies and related fields such as teacher education. Education Studies is an important subject area and should be at the heart of many faculties of education. There is a need for relevant, core texts within Education Studies, which explore and critique contemporary issues across the discipline and challenge prevailing discourses of what education is about. We also need to provide students with strong theoretical perspectives and frameworks, focusing on relevant literature in an accessible and readable format.

We set the authors of this series a number of challenges in terms of what to include in their text. Therefore, each book addresses a contemporary issue in education and has an international rather than just an English focus. The texts are structured to provide a clear grasp of the topic and to provide an overview of research, current debates and perspectives. Contextualized extracts from important primary texts ensure readers' exposure to dominant contemporary theories in the field of education, by demystifying essential vocabulary and educational discourse, enabling the student to engage with these texts in a meaningful way. The extensive and appropriate literature review in each text gives a firm base for contextualizing the subject and promoting understanding at multiple levels.

This series is grounded in a strong conceptual, theoretical framework and is presented in an accessible way. Each book uses features such as case studies, reflective exercises and activities that encourage and support student learning. Key relevant and contemporary questions are inserted throughout each chapter to extend the readers' thinking and understanding. Furthermore, additional material is also provided in the companion website to each book.

Changing Urban Education is the inaugural text in the series Contemporary Issues in Education Studies. It is co-authored by Simon Pratt-Adams, Meg Maguire and Elizabeth Burn. These authors write with the perceptiveness gained from their extensive experience and knowledge of working in urban schools combined with teaching and researching about urban education in universities. They are therefore able to relate school-based to wider forms of theoretical analysis.

The book deals with the changing nature of urban education, exploring the myths and realities of urban lives in the face of new and emerging cultural and social configurations. By acknowledging the complexities of the urban, the book sketches out the potential for real change in a variety of urban settings via local, global and increasingly virtual engagement. The book links this dynamic to issues of policy and critical urban pedagogy from early years to adult education. This critical examination of urban theories, the concept of change and the relationship between urban education policy and practice seeks to move beyond description to actively engage the reader in these ongoing debates. Furthermore, it provides a challenging vision that is optimistic yet grounded, but most importantly is based within a socially just framework.

Changing Urban Education makes an authoritative and constructive contribution towards comprehending the urban setting, urban life and urban education in changing times and will become a major resource for all those who are interested in and care about urban education. It also challenges some of the ways in which urban education has been constructed and understood previously. Crucially, it encourages the reader to think critically and differently about the education that is offered in urban contexts. As the authors of this volume maintain, what is required is not more of the same because for the urban dweller, what has gone before has not worked. What is needed now is a time for new thinking, new hope and new visions in order for *real change* to take place in urban education theory and practice. This book takes up that challenge.

Simon Pratt-Adams and Richard Race
Series Editors
London, January 2010

Acknowledgements

We would like to thank all those who made this book possible.

We are particularly indebted to Sandra Sinfield, Tom Burns and series co-editor Richard Race for their critical feedback and support with the draft manuscript. We would also like to thank Graham Sawyer for proof-reading the text.

We are very grateful to Steve Blum, John Crook, Michael Dunne, Anthony Edwards, Suresh Jethwa, Jeong Sook Lee, Jacqui Pratt-Adams, Bruno Selun and Carl Smith for reading early drafts of different chapters.

Thanks also to Alison Clark and Jo Allcock at Continuum.

Finally, love and thanks to our partners Jacqui, Steve and Michael for their support and encouragement during the writing of this book.

Introduction

The title of this book is, in some ways, deceptively simple. 'Changing Urban Education' can mean just that – changing what goes on in urban schools, although what is meant by an urban school is itself contested and subject to multiple meanings. In this book, we want to deal with the proposition of changing urban education in at least two major ways. First, we want to acknowledge the fluidity, hybridity and change that characterize urban spaces. Cities are not static or 'finished'; they are ongoing projects of transition. One only has to think of cities like Shanghai or Mumbai, to recognize the constant changes that are taking place. In London, New York and Paris, global connectedness, illustrated by constantly changing and increasingly cosmopolitan communities, spurs on the growth and change of these major world cities. Cities are characterized by change; perhaps the real challenge relates to managing this change in ways that are sustainable and equitable.

We have used the word 'change' in the title to signal that we want to challenge some of the older ways in which the city and the urban have sometimes been constructed, specifically in the field of Education Studies. The city and the urban have always been powerful sources for academic study particularly by geographers and sociologists. Those with a particular interest in urban education have sometimes taken up these accounts less critically, to construct a version of the city as a place of dereliction and deficit. Contrasting perspectives, particularly the insights of cultural theorists have tended to see cities more as 'lived complexities' rather than places of darkness and deviancy. These culturalist approaches have not always been influential in education policy and practice. Thus, there are somewhat divergent accounts of the city that draw from these different disciplines to present the urban explorer (who we hope is reading this book) with a dilemma. When the word 'urban' is used, what images are conjured up? Is the urban synonymous with a place of poverty and run down no-go areas? Alternatively, is the city a place of cultural richness, ripe for understanding in a different way – as a place of excitement and enduring fascination, as well as a place of social division and injustice, a place where people can play out their lives in different and complex ways? This book locates the city as a concept that needs to be read through both these approaches. Borrowing from Stevenson's work (2003), our case is that these contrasting approaches can make a powerful contribution towards urban education in repositioning the worlds of the urban learner in a more enabling and hopeful manner.

This book deals with the need to change how urban education is understood. There is a need to move away from deficit versions towards more complex understandings. The book also deals with some of the implications of this reconstruction in terms of changes that could happen in practice. Global interconnectedness as well as a recognition of developing cultural dimensions of urban life call up the possibilities for changes in urban pedagogy and practice, aspects that we address in this volume.

This book is written primarily for all those who are studying for Education Studies degrees with an interest in the urban and urban education, although we hope that others who are concerned with urban schools will find something of value in these chapters. In 2000, the Quality Assurance Agency (QAA) for Higher Education issued its Benchmark Statement for this area of work. It said that:

> Education Studies is concerned with understanding how people develop and learn throughout their lives. It facilitates a study of the nature of knowledge, and a critical engagement with a variety of perspectives, and ways of knowing and understanding, drawn from a range of appropriate disciplines . . . and the cultural, societal, political and historical contexts within which they are embedded. (QAA, 2000: 4 cited in Matheson, 2004: 12)

Education Studies, in this conception, goes beyond what happens in schools; it is much more broadly located. Thus, in this book, we have attempted to provide historical accounts and socio-political analyses that enrich and lend depth to the ways in which the urban is understood. This is because we believe that without an explicit theory of the urban, education practices are less likely to address the central issues (Grace, 2007). We have sometimes used the terms 'urban' and 'city' interchangeably. What we are concerned with is the process by which people come to live and work in large settlements, cities, as well as the cultural forms and experiences that are generated by processes of urbanization (Maguire, Wooldridge and Pratt-Adams, 2006). Thus, sometimes the city is seen as a space, a space that is sometimes defined against the 'rural'. We also explore how, with rapid advances in technology, the spatial and locational designations of the city may be transformed in other respects.

There are two related spatial issues that need to be clarified. Sometimes in this book we talk about UK policy and at other times we talk about English policy approaches as if these were the same. Evidently, this is not the case. There are differences between education policy and provision in Northern Ireland, Scotland, Wales and England and these are not directly addressed in this book. Although we have tried to draw on urban experiences elsewhere, we have mainly focused on the English setting because 'the central dynamic of educational change in post-war Britain, especially since 1979, has been English' (Jones, 2003: 3). We also need to acknowledge another limitation, which is that our work largely concentrates on western cities, although we briefly turn to the social movements in Porto Alegre, Brazil and also make some reference to other world cities.

We have used the word 'change' in our title to signal the need for thinking differently about the education that is offered to working-class children, the education that still seems to fail many working-class children and their families (Ball, 2008). In many of the chapters we have provided a historical perspective in order to address a central matter – that is, what continuities exist in urban education policy and practice and to what extent has there been a change in urban education. In this book we have revisited the work of Paulo Freire and have argued for different approaches towards learning and teaching that really could make a difference in all sectors and at all points in the lifespan. We argue in this volume that urban education policy has frequently been expressed in 'deficit' terms that disregard the impact of the wider social context. There has been a tendency to 'blame' individual children, their parents, their schools and their teachers for any 'failure' in educational attainment. Frequently, education policies designed to ameliorate this outcome have either insisted that children are exposed to more of the curriculum at which they may have already been seen to 'fail'. Alternatively, policies have sometimes been designed that 'select' out those children deemed capable of being 'saved'. Our underlying belief is that despite the policies of neo-liberalism, 'another world is possible. Because of that, another school is possible – and very necessary' (Wrigley, 2006: 10). We hope that this book will contribute towards real change in urban education theory and practice.

Using the book

There are four parts to this book. In the first part we critically theorize and analyse the urban in order to better understand the issues that are to follow. The second part locates urban education in changing times, drawing upon contemporary social and cultural contexts. In the third part we explore education policy-making in practice. Specific learning and teaching practices are considered from the perspective of critical urban educational concerns. Finally we acknowledge the significance of social justice in our arguments and we look forward with complex hope (Grace, 2007) and vision for a more democratic and empowering future for urban education. Each part has its own introduction for easy use and navigation.

At significant points in the book there are activities, which allow the reader to draw upon their knowledge and experiences of the urban against those being raised in the particular section, in order to consider their validity and appropriateness in the context of their own learning. Further reading and useful websites are found at the end of each chapter. There is also an accompanying website that expands and supports the activities found within this book.

There are obviously some omissions in the book. We do not focus specifically on the urban education workforce or teacher education in urban settings, although we believe that much of the book will be relevant to teachers in training. With the exception of the chapter on Early Years education, we have not explicitly considered the separate phases of schooling, although again this is implicit in a number of the chapters.

To describe each chapter in more detail: Chapter 1 explores what is meant by urbanism from a theoretical and conceptual approach. We use a culturalist perspective to consider how the complexities of urban living can be used positively in teaching and learning. Following this, Chapter 2 considers the process of urbanization and how and why urban populations may be constituted as insiders and outsiders in different settings and contexts. Chapter 3 takes a different approach towards theorizing the urban. It explores the urban context physically and virtually in the light of the impact of new and emergent technologies, particularly the internet (Castells, 2000). Chapter 4 presents an exploration of cultural diversity and social justice, especially in relation to the provision of faith schools in urban settings. Chapter 5 broadens the discussion to consider the impact of globalization on urban communities and urban education. This section finishes with Chapter 6 where we review contemporary urban education policies in the UK. We argue that the urban locale can and should be used as a site for promoting a different sort of critical learning.

In the third part, these themes are picked up in Chapter 7 where the link between policy and practice is more fully explored in relation to work on critical pedagogy. This leads on to chapter 8 that concentrates on urban Early Years education as this is a vital element of educational practice, but a phase that has been sometimes neglected in the urban education literature. Chapter 9 returns to the theme of new and emergent technologies and E-learning in relation to urban education practices. Chapter 10 is entitled 'Justice, Hope and Vision' and brings together key themes that have been discussed in previous chapters. We offer some concluding remarks regarding our central concerns of *change in urban education* and *changing urban education*.

Part 1
Theorizing the Urban

In this first part, we examine urbanism and urban living in a multidisciplinary way. Our emphasis here is with the urban experience over time and the ways in which urbanism has been and continues to be structured and represented. We are also interested in constructions of the urban that go beyond spatial boundaries, hence our chapter on the 'virtual' urban. Much of the work on urban education concentrates on issues that relate more directly to the urban classroom and these are topics that we explore in later sections of this book. However, we believe that the field of urban education could be enriched and changed by incorporating a broader approach that includes a culturalist and experiential perspective towards urban living. In the introduction, we argued that Education Studies should involve a critical engagement with a wide range of disciplines including 'the cultural, societal, political and historical contexts within which they are embedded' (QAA, 2000: 4). In this first section, this is what we have attempted to do.

Urban Myths and Urban Lives

Chapter Outline

Introduction

In this first chapter, we want to explore what is meant by urbanism and urban living. Our intention is to go beyond a 'problems' approach towards the city and offer an alternative perspective that challenges and displaces any deficit views. 'There is a whole mythology, or rather demonology, of cities which has led to the view that conflicts multiply with urban growth, according to the scale of urban settlements' (Glass, 2008).

We want to explore and understand the city in an interdisciplinary way, 'seeing the city through diverse eyes' (Landry, 2000: 247) as a place and also as a 'symbolic project' (Zukin, 2003: 146). Our intention is to position the city and urban life as a set of 'wishes and desires, anxieties and fears' (Pile, 2005: 6) as well as places of disruption, consumption, inequality and opportunity. While this approach is well established in cultural theorists' work on the city (Raban, 1974; Donald, 1992; Stevenson, 2003), it has not yet been as widely utilized in the field of urban education studies.

Throughout this chapter and this book, we argue that the city and urban life need to be approached in a way that moves beyond any simple binaries of 'good' or 'bad'. We want to locate and read the city in a way that recognizes the political, the structural and the material realities of urbanization, including the cultural representations and experiences that make up the urban world. There are two reasons for doing this. First, we are concerned that the urban (and urban educational provision) is frequently demonized. In contrast, our aim in this first chapter is to demonstrate that the city is a more complex and enriching resource for teaching and learning than has sometimes been appreciated. Second, we want to broaden the range and scope of urban education through drawing on a culturalist perspective to complement and extend our approach.

The idea of the city: reality, metaphor and imagined project

'How we imagine the city, its boundaries, and the space in which it exists depends largely on what our interest in the city is and what we want to know about it' (Cinar and Bender, 2007: 6). In many ways, the idea of the city is a slippery one. On the one hand, the city can be seen as a place and a 'real thing', but then problems start to creep into this construction in terms of delineating spatially what is, and isn't, urban. If we are thinking about cities within walls, then it is relatively easy to recognize where the city starts and ends. Some cities are spatially defined in this way (Byrne, 2001). However, when we try to consider the boundaries of global cities like Tokyo or London, although we may be able to identify the city centre, its major leisure zones or some key housing areas, it might be another thing to pinpoint where the city ends. In the 'giant social aggregations of our era' (Cinar and Bender, 2007: xi), how do we mark out the city in terms of its space and its borders? Is Yokohama a separate city or a suburb of Tokyo? Is Ealing in London? How do we distinguish between different city forms such as capital cities and regional centres? When we are talking about city life, are we talking about what happens in city centres, at their edges or outside them? What part is played by the specificity of space and place in understanding the city?

In this chapter and in this book, we do not want to lose sight of the spatial and material city, the 'real' city. Indeed, we believe that 'inequalities and exclusions continue to assert their influence in both social and spacial terms' (Chatterton and Hollands, 2003: 11). The city has a physical and material reality, one that plays a fundamental part in distributing and limiting life chances. Some time ago, Pahl (1968) highlighted a distinction between 'proximity' and 'access' in urban settings that helped explain the pattern of resource distribution. He argued that some people were forced to live in less favourable places – in areas where there were factories emitting harmful gases or limited green spaces. These people lived in proximity to reduced life chances and to increased risks. Other people were, and still are, better placed to access social goods because of where they live or because of their capacity to travel to where they can access advantage (Harvey, 1989b). Place and space are crucial in any struggle over consumption. Where you live can dictate which hospital you are treated in, what dentist is available, what school you can attend. Patterns of housing allocation, the availability (or not) of work, transport connections, the accessibility of public-welfare resources, for example, make some places more or less attractive; this inhibits or attracts occupancy and raises or lowers the desirability of any area. But there may be a conflict between where people desire to live and where they want to 'play'. For example, some people may want to experience an edgy, diverse nightlife while living in a risk-free environment. How different people desire to use and consume space and place may be contradictory and fluid and depend on, or be constrained by, their embodied, lived (and spatially influenced) identity (du Gay et al., 2002).

So, while we recognize that space and place have always been powerful factors in the distribution of social goods and opportunities, we also want to consider the ways in which the city works as an idea, as a metaphor and as an imagined project. What we mean by this is that the city is not only a geographical and spatial 'thing', it is also a construction in the popular imagination (Archer et al., 2010). Visualize the New York skyline. This process may then conjure up symbols of capitalism, power and dominance because it is an iconic, internationally recognizable image. What this symbol means to different people and how it is interpreted by them will depend on their politics, their identities and the places where they live. Thus, while the destruction of the Twin Towers in New York City on 11 September 2001 was a 'real' event, it also carried with it, enormous symbolic meanings. One reading of this event is that the Twin Towers

> symbolized a crushing privileging of the global North over the unmodernized scapes of the South. The iconography of Northern wealth was embedded deeply into the artefacts of modernity as embodied in the Twin Towers. Their loss carries an equivalent symbolic and cultural impact. (CPPR, 2002: 313)

Another response to September 11 is to regard the destruction of the Towers as a metaphor for the vulnerability and the transience of urban 'realities' that until this point in time had signalled permanence and domination.

As we have already suggested, there are many different city forms. In terms of UK cities, London, Manchester, Lincoln and Brighton are distinctive and different from one another. In the US, the same is true of cities like Los Angeles, New York and San Diego. There are also 'multiple and heterogeneous ways of experiencing cities' (Bell and Haddour, 2000: 1). These different experiences will be mediated by material and structural differences that in turn will influence patterns of consumption. For instance, the city at night will be differently experienced by diverse social groups. Chatterton and Hollands' (2003) study of UK urban nightscapes details the way in which corporate powers have produced distinctive 'brands' of nightlife, what Chatterton and Hollands call 'pubcos'. Mainstream brewers own, control and run large city-centre, high street located, public houses that cater for younger, relatively wealthier people. These pubs provide live music, special cut-rate deals on alcohol, and sometimes, free entry to women, in order to encourage higher numbers of male customers. These pubcos contrast with other public houses, for example, those located in poorer parts of the city that serve a localized community. While material differences shape the way in which the city is produced and experienced, the ways that individuals position themselves play into these urban experiences. There is space for action and agency in how the city is used or consumed. For example, some students may choose to drink in working-class pubs rather than 'pubcos'. They may see these pubs as more authentic; pubcos might not resonate with who they feel themselves to be; local pubs may simply be cheaper.

In cultural terms, the urban has always been a contradictory phenomenon because cities have been regarded as places of opportunity and innovation, and simultaneously as places of moral degradation, crime and social unrest. The city contains opera houses, major art galleries and theatres. It also provides shelter to many of the homeless who sleep in the doorways of these cultural palaces. This contrast has sometimes resulted in the city being seen in a dichotomized way, as a place of evil and despair contrasted with bright lights and high culture. These dichotomized views themselves are contradictory and contain ambiguities and overlaps. Take for example, this 'real' but very dismal portrait of one form of city life:

> It is necessary only to look into the inner courtyards of a council-house estate, with graffiti on every wall, the windows covered with metal grilles and the doors padlocked, to understand that state of siege in which parts of London still lives. (Ackroyd, 2001: 492)

However, in a different reading, 'tagging' and graffiti (but not the damage and neglect) might be seen as an expression of urban life, a cultural expression of the urban, a work of art and a 'crime of style' (Ferrell, 1993). Again, how these cultural readings are made will depend on the perspectives and situatedness of those who do the decoding and interpretation.

To summarize, what we are suggesting is that the city has a materiality and a structure. It has borders but it also has complex overlays that are spatially located. Simultaneously, it is also an imagined and contested project: 'Real cities are both material constructions, with human strengths and weaknesses, and symbolic projects developed by social representations' (Zukin, 2003: 146).

Activity

Think of a city with which you are familiar.
　Where do young people go for entertainment?
　Where do families like to live?
　Where is the most exciting part of the city?
　Now think about your identity; your age, class, gender, religion, sexuality, with/out children etc. Do these factors affect your answers?

Representing the city

Now we want to consider, in a little more depth, the way in which the city is constructed and represented in the expressive arts. To some degree, we shall be elaborating on some of the points that we have already made in terms of the city as a construct, but, what we want to do is provide some concrete examples of Zukin's 'symbolic projects developed by social representations'. Before we attempt this, there is a good deal of research and writing that deals with this subject (Clarke, 1997; Frisby, 2001; Alsayyad, 2006) and so, in what follows, we will only be able to provide an indicative and descriptive account of some parts of this complex and wide-ranging area of work. Perhaps the 'best' place to start is with an expression that has been used almost excessively in relation to the city – the city of night, of darkness and despair. To some degree, there is the almost inevitable dichotomy between urban decay and rural regeneration that is mirrored in many forms of the expressive arts. A strong contrast between urban night and rural light can be traced in paintings, poetry and even in music over time. One of the most 'celebrated' representations of urban life comes from the poem 'The City of Dreadful Night' by James Thompson (1880).

> The City is of Night, but not of Sleep;
> There sweet sleep is not for the weary brain;
> The pitiless hours like years and ages creep,
> A night seems termless hell. This dreadful strain
> Of thought and consciousness which never ceases,
> Or which some moments' stupor but increases,
> This, worse than woe, makes wretches there insane.

Different workings of the title of this poem have been used for many short stories (Rudyard Kipling and others), poems, films and academic papers and books. Many of the academic books and papers use reworkings of 'The City of Dreadful Night' in an ironic style in their titles, although some of the poems, films and stories deal in a more straightforward and literal manner with the alienation and 'horror' that is often central in representations of urban life. For example, consider the persistence of the tales of Jack the Ripper in London's East End or the tales of Sweeney Todd, the demon barber. Dickens' novels frequently feature urban contrasts where there is a vile, degrading environment that symbolizes the threat to the main protagonist and, if it does not end in death, there is usually a redemptionist ending in an 'appropriate' setting. Think of Oliver Twist living in a wretched dwelling when he unwittingly becomes part of Fagin's criminal activities. Compare this with the bliss he experiences when Mr Brownlow takes him up to live as a cherished member of his household, and ultimately, as one of the Brownlow family. This powerful, sustained and almost one-dimensional representation of the urban situates the city (and London in particular) as 'dark' and alienating, as a place of risk, danger and potential corruption, although there is potential for being rescued from this setting.

Williams (2000: 60) believes that in many of the cultural representations of the urban 'a direct relationship is proposed between the city and a form of agonized consciousness'. He writes of the representation of the dark London of the nineteenth century where the city is a 'teeming, mazelike, often alien area' containing 'warrens of crime' (p. 61). Much of the literature of the nineteenth century and early twentieth century deals with the urban setting in this way. However, to what degree has this stereotype been sustained over time? Here it is useful to consider the way in which stories of the London life and times of a fictional, cocaine-using solver of pernicious and foul crimes, Sherlock Holmes, have persisted. Currently, there are museums and city walks and a massive Sherlock Holmes industry that contributes towards making this character almost a 'real' person. Perhaps the same is true of Sweeney Todd, another mythical figure who is constantly 'remembered' and 'reinvented' in song, film, waxwork museums and other tourist centres in the city and whose life is deeply bedded into the alleyways and darknesses at the mythic 'heart' of London. Our point here is *not* to displace the structural and material *reality* of poverty and oppressions that have patterned and continue to shape the urbanized world; we want to briefly account for the way in which the 'urban' has been *represented*, and continues to be represented in the expressive arts. These representations then get taken up and amplified by powerful groups, for example the media and political groups, who use them as part of what Archer et al. (2010: 7) call 'the ongoing history of the pathologization of urban space'.

When we turn to the ways in which cities are portrayed in film, there is a complexity and diversity that defies any easy generalizations, although there are specific genres of film that take up representations of the city and urban life in particular ways. The city itself variously works as a metaphor for sophistication, civilization, urbanity and culture. It also signals evil, loss of morality, lasciviousness, and repeatedly, loss and darkness – and sometimes both at the same time. Some films deal more directly with versions of urban lives and the urban world. Although we do not have enough space to deal with this specific matter more fully, it would be intriguing to trace the various, and stereotyped ways, in which social class has been delineated in film. The same is true of gendered and racialized identities. Some films such as *My Beautiful Laundrette* do attempt to portray the complex classed, 'raced' and gendered hybrid identities of a small group of Londoners. 'By leaving the usual symbols of London out of the film, *My Beautiful Laundrette*, also presents London as a decidedly postcolonial city' (Alsayyad, 2006: 205). *Dirty Pretty Things* presents a similar perspective. This film eschews the 'usual' London symbols of Big Ben or the Houses of Parliament to tell a story of asylum seekers and a market in body organs in the city. Other films concentrate on a glossy, surreal cosmopolitan (and nearly all-white and middle class) London. For example, *Notting Hill* and *Four Weddings and a Funeral* (just remember the rural–urban contrasts) fit neatly into this category.

But there are other genres and other categories too. Think of the 'lurid' city as represented in the films of the 1950s (Shaw, 1997) and the dystopic visions of the city in films such as *Alphaville* to *Bladerunner* through to the more recent *Sin City*. These diverse filmic representations of the city articulate different sets of narratives that go beyond most individual experiences. If the cinema is 'an alternative public space where individuals can develop a new sense of themselves' (Emden et al., 2006: 18) and the places where they live and work, then these films offer contrasting versions of the city that may contribute towards stereotypes and myths. At their best and most innovative, they project unexpected and unrecognized articulations of different dimensions of urban living that in turn produce new myths and new representations.

One of the more longstanding genres that draws on the cityscape as metaphor, site and symbol for its sustenance is the detective story. Crime thrillers are often located in cities, whether it be the American cities of the 1940s and 1950s films, or the 'dark' London of the nineteenth century. Turning to the contemporary crime thriller, just visualize Rebus' Edinburgh, Robicheaux' New Orleans, V. I. Warshawski's Chicago or even Sam Spade's San Francisco, the list is endless. In these narratives, the central importance of the city as a symbol and metaphor becomes clear. As Bershady (2007: 70) has pointed out, the detective solving a mystery in the city 'reveals the city as part of the mystery'. In contrast, he suggests that the small-town detective who solves a crime is 'restoring the town's innocence'. Thus, 'the city always remains to be detected' (Frisby, 2001: 99).

One more point and one more genre – that relates directly to urban education. It would be useful to critically review those films that deal with urban schooling in greater depth, as this has been and continues to be a popular theme in film making. As Archer et al. (2010: 6) point out, many of the Hollywood movies about urban schools are racialized redeptionist accounts where 'White teachers are positioned as "saviours" and White students are largely absent from representations of urban schools'. These accounts are also intersected by social class in various ways; either as 'the site of multi-ethnic working class gang-warfare and drug-taking' or, as in the case of films located in northern England, locked into a 'nostalgia for a lost, industrial, Northern and mostly White, working class past' (Archer et al., 2010: 6).

Overall then, what we are suggesting in this part is that it is useful to see the city as a set of representations that are open to different interpretations and contested readings (Westwood and Williams, 1996). We have already suggested that some of the research that explores urban educational provision could be enhanced by an appreciation of the 'work' that is being done through and by these representations. This is because 'the images we have of the city can influence how it is experienced both consciously and unconsciously' (Dobson, 2007: 169).

Activity

What different representations of the city are you aware of – in soaps, in literature, in films and books.
  How are urban working-class communities represented?

The city as a social, cultural and economic resource

Our discussion so far sketches out some of the ways in which the city has been a resource, at least in film, literature and other expressive forms of representation. Now we want to review some other ways in which the city acts as a resource. Cities are marketed in order to be attractive and desirable to specific constituencies. The intention is that businesses will then locate in cities and tourism will be enhanced and expanded. The drawing in of multi-national corporations, banks and other finance-sector industries to locations in various city centres is, in part, made an 'attractive' proposition through various government schemes that off-set taxes and make the city an even more desirable setting for relocation. In order to attract and maintain businesses and industries in city locations, the city has to market itself. (Thus, cities are constructed as the loci of industry and this can act as a repressive force on some urban inhabitants as we shall see in the next chapter).

One part of this marketization relates to developing the city through major and sometimes internationally renowned projects such as innovative architecture and buildings; the 'Birds Nest' of Beijing, the 2008 Olympic Stadium, is a good example of this type of innovation. Another part of the marketing of cities relates to the reworking of older buildings that become reassigned in the post-industrial city; for example, the Tate Modern in London was transformed from a disused power station to an international art gallery. Most post-industrialized cities now have waterside areas that were once used as docklands, but that have been transformed into small businesses, city housing, design studios, galleries and wine bars, frequently named in ways that call up their previous existence, for example the Albert Dock in Liverpool and Canary Wharf in London (Maguire, Wooldridge and Pratt-Adams, 2006). In these projects, cultural planning and urban design have been worked together to provide spectaculars, play sites as well as post-industrial workspaces for the economically mobile twenty-first century citizen.

Particularly in the global post-industrialized cities like New York, Tokyo and London (Sassen, 2006), but also in regional cities like Manchester, Chicago and Melbourne, older areas are being reclaimed and gentrified. Most cities will have centres, and sometimes sets of centres, that contain provision for leisure events, one-off activities (the London Aquarium and London Eye) as well as specialist sports centres and shopping areas that are pedestrianized. There may be large screen cinemas (Imax) as well as international cuisine, a multiplicity of music venues, theatres and clubs all available in a small walkable area of the city. All these resources will be called up in the kaleidoscope of images that are superimposed to construct a representation of the city as a centre of privatized and individualized consumption and desire.

In the twentieth century, particularly in the US, suburbanization became a dominant and aspirational lifestyle (Wiese, 2005; Jackson, 2007). The city centre was, in the main, a daytime place of work which was evacuated at night and those who continued to live in the city were, in the main, those who could not make the transition to the suburbs. By the 1960s, a pattern of urban gentrification started to emerge in the US and in the UK. 'Fuelled by the baby-boomers who were better educated, more prosperous and had larger disposable incomes than their parents' generation, the city became an arena of conspicuous consumption' (Maguire, Wooldridge and Pratt-Adams, 2006: 3). Suburban housing that afforded easy access to the city was expensive and transport costs high, so that young professionals now turned to 'improving neighbourhoods' within the city. This move was driven by 'positive images of city-living based on a deep dislike of suburban environments' (Savage and Warde, 1993: 85). Urban gentrification meant buying up older properties, often in run-down and edgy areas, restoring them and adding significantly to their value, while pushing their price beyond what was affordable for the indigenous working-class communities. Gentrification was a movement of 'the middle class replacing the working class; increasing property values; alteration in the built environment and the emergence of a new urban style of life' (Savage and Warde, 1993: 80).

Activity

What are the benefits and what are the costs of gentrification?

In the second half of the twentieth century and persisting into the twenty-first, parts of inner cities have become stylish, desirable places in which to work, live and consume. Land prices and property prices have risen accordingly, so the city has become a powerful economic, social and cultural resource, despite the 'credit crunch'. This has propelled different people with diverse interests and commitments towards the city, although others have been pushed outwards by this particular movement of people. The resources that are on offer in a city, with its critical mass of diverse and cosmopolitan people, mean that urban settings offer possibilities and potential for creativity and originality that may not be available elsewhere.

However, there is a fundamental contradiction that is posed by the city as a resource – whether this be social, cultural or economic. The possibility of what seems like a more interesting and advantageous lifestyle, a new identity, may well work to attract people towards the city but the reality is that some will be better placed than others to access and consume these 'dominant' resources. One consequence may be the production and generation of alternative forms of urban consumption; for instance, the squatters movements that still exist in some parts of cities; the growing allotment movement; co-operative markets; thrift shops and other community-based activities. However, these alternative lifestyles may only offer alternatives and choices for those who are already privileged. Somewhat ironically, these 'alternative' resources may work to further shore up the diversity and spectacle of the city; thus street markets, festivals and other alternative cultural expressions will be caught up and represented in the marketing and image-making of the city.

> . . . within the new kind of open, complex and mobile society, small groups in any form of divergence and dissent could find some kind of foothold, in ways that would not have been possible if the artists and thinkers composing them had been scattered in more traditional closed societies. (Williams, 2000: 63)

In an individualistic and consumerist society, this 'complex and mobile society', where what you consume is who you are, Sennett (1990) has claimed that urban spaces have become segmented in terms of housing and leisure use. Materially advantaged people will live in gated homes with private security guards. They will cross the city in cars that effectively seal them off from any contact with 'others'. They will work, shop, eat and 'play' in offices, restaurants, clubs and environments that are only available to people like themselves. Young professionals may socialize in 'achingly cool' spots, but will do this largely with similar cohorts. 'Middle-class unease' about the presence of 'the poor and the marginal' (Stevenson, 2003: 45) in common open places like streets and parks has led to segregation where some desirable spaces are heavily controlled to 'manage' entrance. Other spaces become evacuated and avoided by the same middle-class groups in an attempt to avoid the 'other'. Thus, the urban becomes fragmented in relation to 'access' and 'proximity' factors located in the material 'real city'. So, while parts of the city become reworked and refurbished as centres for industry, leisure and tourism, they are also shaped to exclude and reduce the visibility of the poor, of those who are 'othered'. In his study of the urban ghettos of Paris and Chicago, Wacquant (2007) talks of 'stigmatized neighbourhoods' and 'advanced marginality'. This is as much a spatial as a symbolic process. So, in this first chapter, while we want to ensure that the city is understood as a metaphor and a representation, we want to stress that this perspective complements the structural and material realities of urban life.

Theorizing the urban

At this point, it seems useful to outline briefly what we understand by 'the urban'. Saunders (1986: 7) states that in the UK 'the boundaries between city and countryside, urban and rural are generally indistinct'. He argues that while place is part of what is meant by the urban, what is distinctive are questions which are 'basic to the sociological analysis of advanced capitalist societies' (Saunders 1981: 278). There are similarities between urban and rural settings; poverty and disadvantage are not just evident in cities. However, the crucial point is that 'Metropolitan cities provide the arenas for the making visible of fundamental contradictions within the wider society and of the ideological and political conflicts associated with such contradictions' (Grace, 1978: 3). This understanding lies at the heart of the analysis of the urban which underpins the work in this book. It is these 'fundamental contradictions' which need to be recognized, and which are intensified in urban settings. However, we would want to bring in a perspective that includes cultural representations and experiences as part of this analysis, as these constructions fuel the popular imagination and pattern socio-political policies and practices, as we shall see in other chapters in this book.

Education in the city

Finally, in this chapter, we want to start to discuss the part that education plays in constructing the city in general terms and in relation to what Thrift (2000: 250) calls 'the learning cities of knowledge, identity and soft capitalism'. Later on in this book, we will be considering aspects of education policy and provision in a more specifically educational manner. Here we want to point out that cities are great storehouses of knowledge and experience, from their diverse populations to the 'pedagogic institutions from schools to museums to libraries, (that) are scattered through them' (Thrift, 2000: 250). Indeed, the educational assets and educational goods that are more evident in city spaces work to construct and position the city as a desirable location and a setting for identity transformation. People move to cities to access formal educational opportunities, improve their life chances and remake themselves in different ways (Byrne, 2001).

But the city is also a space and place for other sorts of learning, learning that is critical, culturally and expressively focused, socially and welfare-driven as well as much more. Landry (2000: 267) argues that we are living in a period of rapid and 'unprecedented' change that 'erodes the possibility of ever recovering the traditions of stability'. He points out that the twenty-first century will be 'the century of cities' (Landry, 2000: xiii); over half the world now live in cities, and in Europe, this rises to 75 per cent of the population. Thus, there is a need to ensure that cities are positive places in which to live and learn. His response to this pressing need is to argue for capitalizing on creative learning that harnesses the capabilities of diverse groups and that sees diversity and differences as a potential and not a liability. 'The learning city is . . . strategic. Creative, imaginative and intelligent – it looks at its potential resources in a far more comprehensive way . . . it turns weaknesses into strengths, it makes something out of nothing' (Landry, 2000: 267).

This approach needs to be situated in relation to how cities are presently constructed in terms of relations of power and class. For instance, there are increased 'divisions between rich and poor in the new London' (Hamnett, 2003: 248) as elsewhere (Wacquant, 2007). When we are dealing more specifically with urban education, and by this we mean the schooling of the urban working classes, any account has to recognize the cultural and situate it in an understanding of the structural and material context.

Conclusion

What we have tried to do in this chapter is look at some of the different ways in which the city has been and continues to be represented. We believe there is a need to be alert to the ways in which representations and 'fictional accounts blur into factual ones' (Archer et al., 2010: 7). This is because these representations are taken up, repeated and reworked into stories of the city that can then work powerfully on our conscious and subconscious understandings of the urban and urban life to demonize and further exclude working-class families. What we have also tried to do in this chapter is to provide some theoretical resources for reading the city. These will be deployed in this book in order to consider urban educational theory and practices and ask different sorts of questions about the urban world, urban lives and urban education.

Further reading

Jayne, M. (2006) *Cities and Consumption*. London: Routledge.

Massood, P. J. (2003) *Black City Cinema: African American Urban Experiences in Film*. Philadelphia: Temple University Press.

Neal, L. (2000) *Victorian Babylon: People, Streets, and Images in Nineteenth-century London*. New Haven: Yale University Press.

Shiel, M. and Fitzmaurice, T. (eds) (2001) *Cinema and the City: Film and Urban Societies in a Global Context*. Oxford: Blackwell.

Useful websites

http://www.brookings.edu/metro/living-cities/main.aspx

The Brookings Institute publishes a fascinating 'Living Cities Census Series' about US urban areas at:

http://www.bestplaces.net/City/

You can compare many cities in terms of some key variables on City Compare

Peopling the City

Introduction

The first chapter explored the ways in which, while the city exists as a material form, as 'bricks and mortar', it is also a construction of the imagination and of the psyche. In this second chapter, we turn to another way in which the city can be 'read'. Here we explore the ways in which the city has been historically constructed, and continues to be reconstructed, by those who inhabit the city. In this chapter, we consider the people of the city as being constituted as insiders and outsiders. Insiders are those who have access to social goods and advantage, those who know how the system works and who have the capacity to reproduce social advantage for themselves and their families. In contrast, outsiders are less able to access social advantage. In exploring the experiences of insiders and outsiders, while there are specific contexts in which exclusions are clearly delineated, and socio-economic settings would be one of these, there are other arenas where this division may be differently sculpted. Being an insider/outsider is a shifting construction and can be differently constituted in different contexts and settings.

This chapter starts by outlining the process of urbanization and detailing some of its consequences in terms of social divisions and exclusions. Our point is to demonstrate that, right from the start, the city was built on oppressions and exclusions that have always been delineated in socio-economic terms and reflected in housing, occupations and welfare provision. However, although material and structural divisions exist in the city, there are other differences that make up the identities of city dwellers in different ways. In briefly exploring some of the ways in which the city is experienced, we argue that identity plays a part in patterning inclusion and exclusion. Finally, we explore the ways in which patterns of inclusion and exclusion have worked, and continue to work, in and on the urban educational setting.

Urbanization and its consequences

As we have argued elsewhere, one way of understanding 'the urban' is to regard it as 'a condensate for the consequences of urbanization, a process that has been and continues to be driven by changes in production' (Maguire, Wooldridge and Pratt-Adams, 2006: 1). In the eighteenth- and nineteenth-century northern hemisphere cities, changes in production modes fuelled the large-scale movements of people. The factories and mechanized workshops that were located in the towns and cities of Britain provided an irresistible pull (available work, wages and an escape from rural poverty) that was also propelled or 'pushed' in some part by changes in agricultural methods and the Land Enclosure Acts. These Acts had taken away rights of access to lands that could be used for grazing stock. The enclosures dealt a final blow to many tenant farmers and rural agricultural workers who relied on this free resource in order to survive. For many rural workers this was the final impetus for moving to a new way of life and a new way of earning a living in the rapidly expanding urban centres (Neeson, 1993).

Many people were compelled to move to towns and cities to seek employment, bringing their families with them. There was no alternative but to starve or migrate. The newly emerging business and entrepreneurial classes saw this growing throng of internal (and external) migrants as a cheap form of expendable labour. Their responsibilities only extended to paying a wage; any ill-health or reasons that removed workers from the labour market and thus removed their capacity to earn a living were to be assuaged by appeals to charity, the poor laws and the workhouse. Thus, the 'rise' of the city was characterized by the emergence of two new social classes. There were those who owned the means of employment such as the factory owners and those that sold their labour in these, and similar, establishments for a daily wage – the working classes. By 1861, in Britain, 'the world's first urbanised society' (Byrne, 2001: 6), the majority of the population lived in cities that were characterized by these stark divisions of insiders and outsiders.

The unprecedented scale of migration towards the city inevitably put pressure on a wide range of social provisions. Housing was in short supply and rents could not be paid unless a wage was being brought into the family. The housing stock that was available to rent was frequently of poor quality. Overcrowding in working-class areas was endemic; sanitary provision was limited. Thus, disease and ill health in the homes of the newly urbanized workers was commonplace. For example, in 1842, Friedrich Engels came to work for a textile company based in Manchester in which his father owned shares. He was shocked and distressed by the poverty and deprivations that he witnessed. It is worth considering what he wrote in some detail (see also Stedman-Jones (1971) and Fishman's (1988) accounts of poverty and distress in London):

> Right and left a multitude of covered passages lead from the main street into numerous courts, and he who turns in thither gets into a filth and disgusting grime, the equal of which is not to be found – especially in the courts which lead down to the Irk, and which contain unqualifiedly the most horrible dwellings which I have yet beheld. In one of these courts there stands directly at the entrance, at the end of the covered passage, a privy without a door, so dirty that the inhabitants can pass into and out of the court only by passing through foul pools of stagnant urine and excrement. This is the first court on the Irk above Ducie Bridge – in case any one should care to look into it. Below it on the river there are several tanneries which fill the whole neighbourhood with the stench of animal putrefaction. Below Ducie Bridge the only entrance to most of the houses is by means of narrow, dirty stairs and over heaps of refuse and filth. (Engels, 1892: 45)

In *The Condition of the Working-Class in England in 1844* Engels detailed the squalor and deprivations that characterized working-class life in Manchester. There was a form of housing segregation based on social class patterns, a pattern that was not always evident to those in more privileged circumstances. As Engels noted:

> The town itself is peculiarly built, so that a person may live in it for years, and go in and out daily without coming into contact with a working-people's quarter or even with workers, that is, so long as he confines himself to his business or to pleasure walks. This arises chiefly from the fact, that by unconscious tacit agreement, as well as with outspoken conscious determination, *the working people's quarters are sharply separated from the sections of the city reserved for the middle-class*. (Engels, 1892: 45, *our italics*)

This classed housing segregation that patterned parts of the cities of the nineteenth century occurred alongside a movement out of the cities of many of the middle classes who 'sought to insulate themselves, and especially their wives and children, from the uncouth and possibly dangerous life of the street' (Davidson, 1994: 101, cited in Stevenson, 2003: 18). The segmented and segregated labour force that now took up residence in the poorest, cheapest and most run-down districts accomplished the 'rise' of the industrializing city.

While there were powerful discourses that spoke of the dark and threatening city, and while there were moves by the middle classes to 'escape' into the suburbs, the city was also a place where desires could potentially be fulfilled. It was a place that offered 'escape' from the pressures of work, family and duty. For the middle-class male, this could include access to the prostitution of children and women (Bartley, 1999). For the working classes, the 'escape' might be found in the gin shops of Dickensian London. The anonymity of the city also provided opportunities for homosexuals to meet and form relationships that were outlawed in wider society (Kaplan, 2005). So, then as now, there were also those who wanted to experience or take solace from the excitement, promise, danger, risk and anonymity that the urban presented.

Activity

What 'escapes' exist in the contemporary city – who participates in these activities? Are they inclusive or segregated?

Understanding the city – identity and difference

The urban experience has been theorized in different ways since the city became a focus for scholarly attention. The first major approach to understanding the city was undertaken by the Chicago School in the 1920s and 1930s, led by Robert Park and Louis Wirth. The Chicago School saw the city as designed by patterns and rules that could be 'discovered' and mapped out. For example, it was claimed that cities were zoned in relation to their use: the central business zone and the red light zone. Transition zones buffered some of the more fixed zones. Next to the central business district there would be transition zones of cheap housing and high population density because of easy access to the key zone of prosperity and employment (Park et al., 1925). This proximity allowed for mobility and growth in the city as a consequence of what the Chicago School identified as waves of competition, invasions and successions, a pattern that was also evident in the East End of London (Fishman, 1988). The Chicago School mapped out American cities and studied the way of life that characterized particular locales, concentrating on detailed ethnographic studies of urban subcultures (Wirth, 1928) and the life stories of gangs and other urban dwellers (Thrasher, 1927; Cressey, 1932). This focus on the urban 'way of life' recognized difference and diversity, although it was less critical of the market forces that had produced and sustained this phenomenon. The Chicago School concentrated on the ways in which new migrant communities settled in and adapted to urban life although 'often these adaptations were undermined by the power of economic forces to disrupt social relations and re-sort people not in terms of their communities but rather in terms of the community of money' (Bridge, 2005: 4).

In contrast, theoretical approaches in the 1960s took a more political and economic perspective towards understanding the city. Marxist urban sociologists like Castells (1972), and later on critical urban geographers like Harvey (1973), brought a sharp and new perspective to urban studies. In brief, the social relations of urbanism were taken as 'the cultural expressions of the capitalist mode of production' (Stevenson, 2003: 33). Cities were spatial settings in which the contradictions of capitalism were most visible (Castells, 1972). Urban sociology considered the impact and influence of macro-economic shifts within the capitalist mode of production and its outcomes of inequality and lack of social justice that produced insiders and outsiders.

This approach, that sidelined the social and the cultural, was interrupted by the contribution of (second wave) feminism in the 1970s and onwards. Although explanations of the city that rested on economic and political theorizations were not displaced, what occurred was a refocusing on the cultural, the social and the specific, particularly in terms of the use of space. Feminists were concerned to explain the absence of people, and particularly the absence of women, from urban policy and planning (Massey, 1984). Political and economic approaches towards the city had not dealt with or 'explained' the ways in which the urban was experienced differently because of the lived identities of different people. Greed (1987) talked of the ways in which the city was 'zoned' in gendered terms and argued that women were frequently excluded and marginalized by the way in which space was managed. (Although Greed did not want to contribute to an essentializing binary round the construction of all men as oppressive and all women as subordinate, to some extent this was always a 'risk' in some of the work of the second-wave feminists who were challenging male dominance and patriarchal relations, both spatial and structural).

Feminists working in the field of urban studies argued that city spaces were differently used by women and men (Watson, 1988). For example, changes in housing policy meant that, in the 1980s, the promotion of home ownership and the positioning of suburban housing as highly desirable, but resulted in many mothers who resided in suburban areas having reduced access to a wider range of better paid and higher status occupations. What seemed to be emerging in these locales was what Greed called 'a spatial sub-urban harem away from the city of man' (Greed, 1987: 12). She also pointed out that women were 'encouraged' to fear the city, particularly the 'dangerous' and ill-lit areas of the city at night (Greed, 1994). All of this work was pointing to a differentiated use of space and the city where there were gendered outsiders and insiders. And while the example of women in the suburbs concentrated on the experiences of middle-class women in the main, in the city scape, the story related to all women who allegedly needed to fear the city at night.

More recently, gender theory has shifted away from some of these earlier, perhaps more essentialized categories of 'men' and 'women'. As Bondi (1998: 178) claims, 'gender is far more complex'. Gender is now generally positioned in contemporary scholarship as a fluid and hybrid construction and is made up in different ways by class, 'race'/ethnicity, for example. In this reconstituted approach to gender, that draws on intersectionalities of class and race, as well as other identities, what does this mean in terms of the use of space and place and urban lifestyles? However, what second-wave feminist theory did do in terms of understanding the urban was to make a forceful argument for a need to extend structural and material analyses through drawing on the lived experiences of real people.

Activity

Can you identify examples of some ways in which urban space is more or less accessible to different groups such as women, those with 'disabilities', older people, the young, those on low incomes, etc.?

More recently, there has been a renewed interest in ethnographic and postmodern accounts of city life that focus on aspects of differences, particularly in patterns of consumption (Miles and Hall, 2003; Miles, 2007). In these studies, there is an exploration of urban life and urban lifestyles in producing the city. Although we cannot here do justice to the full range and complexity of these research projects for there are many. For example, as Byrne (2001: 124) explains 'sexual orientation is now an important organising principle of local specialisation in consumption'. Many cities have established lesbian, gay, bisexual and transgender 'zones'. Byrne (2001) argues that these zones are related to consumption use rather than housing – clubs, restaurants, clothing outlets, bars and bookshops – although he suggests that the Castro in San Francisco is an example of both consumption and housing zone. Byrne also claims that cities are divided up according to many different and interrelated aspects of cultural lifestyles and identities. For example, he argues that age/experience can shape the use of space and gives, as an example, the case of student housing areas in urban centres. However, he points to a distinction between different cities in different national settings in relation to racial/ethnic identities. Northern American cities, for instance, are racially segregated and in particular, the segregation of African Americans 'is so culturally and institutionally ingrained' that he believes that the development of a black urban middle class will not influence this pattern to any great degree (Byrne, 2001: 123). In contrast, the cities of the UK are more ethnically heterogeneous, although there are some 'locales of concentration' (p. 124).

In terms of 'reading' the city through the lens of those who *people the city*, and from a perspective that recognizes identity and difference, three key points emerge. First, this viewpoint displaces any over-determinist accounts about a fixed and stable notion of identity; the experiences of all 'women' or all 'men'. People will be constructed, and will construct their complex, shifting and hybrid identities in different ways in different places. Second, cities will attract a diverse population, as they always have done. Thus, cities will be cosmopolitan and characterized by diversity. 'Cities are places where difference is both created and most likely to be tolerated' (Stevenson, 2003: 41). In terms of the urban space itself, the same spatial area may be subjected to different uses at different times of the day (and night). Moreover, this culturalist approach to 'reading' the urban, and peopling the urban, may be hidden from view if the dominant reading is only made through the lens of politics and economics.

So far, we are suggesting that to view the urban solely as an outcome of changes in the modes of production may marginalize alternative readings. The Chicago School approach towards urban lifestyles and subcultural groups explored diversity and difference, but without a political account of these phenomena. What needs to be recovered is a structural *and* cultural account of the part that differences and identities can play in maintaining the divided city – the city of insiders, outsiders, bystanders and those who are teetering on the borders of these positions.

Difference in the city – divisions in the city

Jacobs and Fincher (1998: 1) believe that issues of identity and difference pose some crucial questions in terms of how the city is theorized. As they say: '"The City" as an object of analysis has been irredeemably unsettled, and many of the more resilient ways urban processes are understood have been rendered problematic'. They argue that 'reading' the city through the lenses of identity and difference does not jettison a politics of the urban through 'joyously indulging in urban diversity' (p. 2). Instead, this approach foregrounds some of the messiness and complexity in the geographies of the city. Approaching the lived and peopled city through difference and diversity does not sideline questions of who has access to social goods and who does not. What it does add, in their view, is a recognition of 'the ways in which such structures are, in turn, shaped by the contingent circumstances of specific people in specific settings' (Jacobs and Fincher, 1998: 2). This is not just to draw in a cultural studies approach towards the urban; it is, as they say, an attempt to 'recast the culture-economic dichotomy into a far more powerful cultural political economy of urban identities and places' (p. 3). What this means is that the city and the urban become exposed to a more complex, nuanced and yet difficult set of readings.

Take for example the issue of inaccessibility that has been already discussed in relation to (some) women in the city. Inaccessibility is also part of the economic 'geography of disability' (Gleeson, 1998). Inaccessibility can also pattern the urban experiences of younger urban dwellers. Specific differences produce specific oppressions and exclusions in particular places. To this extent, the urban dweller can be either an insider or outsider or vacillate between both positions, depending on identity and context. Travelling on the London Underground can sometimes be hard to access and perhaps is sometimes threatening when it is late at night and people are coming home from clubbing. A more contextualized approach towards the urban helps to unsettle any easy generalizations about insiders and outsiders and recognizes the role of specificity, place and contingency. It also raises questions about the particularities and peculiarities of the local within the urban. In this way, older urban concerns about production and consumption can now be 'productively complicated' (Jacobs and Fincher, 1998: 22).

In terms of identity, difference and inequality, the city is a spatial centre of diversity and difference, as it has always been (Engels, 1892; Fishman, 1988). But cities are not just spatially formed enclaves divided off from the non-urban, the rural or the suburban. They are peopled, socialized and culturalized, sometimes in distinctive ways. For example, compare the highly segregated 'ghettos' of the North American cities with the 'raced'/ethnic patterns of housing and cultural locales in the English cities (Byrne, 2001; Wacquant, 2007). However, while there are segregations and divisions in the cosmopolitan 'city of difference', Bridge (2005: 158) claims that there are also moments when 'strangers are brought together' and there is 'at least the sight of difference' at specific moments in time (Bridge, 2005: 152). He cites the mobilization of New Yorkers who stood on the streets grieving after 9/11 as well as the vigil of more than eight million people in Spain who stood silently in the city streets after the 11/3 train bombing in Madrid. Yet, on other occasions, as Stevenson (2003: 47) says,

> Cities . . . are becoming places where far from encountering difference, people actively contrive to avoid it. Different social classes, increasingly, are forced to follow different trajectories through space . . . and rarely, if ever, do they encounter the 'other'.

Stevenson cites Davis' claim in 'Cities of Quartz', his study of Los Angeles, that many of us now live in 'fortress cities' divided into 'fortified' areas and 'places of terror' (Davis, 1990: 224, in Stevenson, 2003: 45). Although Stevenson recognizes that gated estates with their own security guards and homes protected by complex sets of alarms, bars and safety devices are perhaps more common in the North American city, nevertheless, this is a tendency that is echoed in some of the more prosperous areas of other Northern Hemisphere cities. The growth of privatized space and the reduction in public assets, such as local swimming pools, local authority controlled libraries and sports facilities signals a divided city – one that is divided by economics. Stevenson (2003: 50) believes that 'issues of personal identity, consumption and lifestyle are replacing commitments to once-fundamental collective objectives and priorities, in particular, those of the relations of production'. Clearly then, in the city of difference, who gets more and who gets less is shaped in part by identity and difference – but it is also shaped by political and economic decisions, policies and practices. As Wacquant (2007) has argued, many contemporary policies that are inflected by racialized and market-oriented discourses are producing patterns of 'advanced marginality' in cities like Paris and Chicago. While it would be a mistake simply to take the city as an expression of capitalist relations, it would equally be a mistake not to do so.

Perhaps, as Stevenson (2003) believes, the issue is not about the *differences* of identities that 'people the city' but its *inequalities* and injustices. In this perspective, understanding the city involves recognizing and respecting the many complex and interwoven differences, the hybrid and flexible multiple identities that people the cosmopolitan city. Individual identities are flexible and hybrid and may become more or less emphasized in different contexts; there are times and spaces where being male or female may be more or less important and where other aspects of identity may shape the lived experience. For instance, sometimes being older can be an asset, regardless of any other dimension of identity. At other times, being positioned as older can be used to exclude and 'other' (Maguire, 2008).

The city offers the space and the scope for some possibility of identity reconstruction where individuals can remake who they are and who they want to be. For example, the anonymity of the city makes possible some space for more transgressive sexualities while simultaneously maintaining hetero-sexist assumptions (Brown, 2000). But this space for identity work, as with everything else, is sharply bounded by power and class. As we have high-lighted, the city is a place of divisions and inequalities and exclusions. For example, London has high levels of poverty and exclusion and 'levels of disadvantage coexist with some of the greatest concentrations of wealth in Great Britain' (Livingstone, 2003).

Insiders and outsiders: an educational dimension

So far, we have been considering the ways in which the city is experienced in terms of identity constructions and differences. This is where education and educational provision come into the story of peopling the city. Education plays a pivotal and somewhat contradictory part in social reproduction and social reconstruction (Fitz et al., 2006). For example, schools can choose to play a major part in supporting and respecting difference, through the formal cur-riculum provision and through the organizational and managerial processes of the school. In this way, schools can become influential spatial settings where children and young people positively engage and interact with aspects of diver-sity and difference as part of their daily lived experience. Through these shared experiences of difference and diversity, children can come to challenge stereo-typing and some of the limits of normalized identity-formations, such as essentialized or traditional constructions of gender roles. In this way it can be possible to 'change some of the excluding practices and identifications that cause so much pain and harm in schools and society' (Maguire, Wooldridge and Pratt-Adams, 2006: 98). However, schools can also ignore the ways that some differences are disrespected 'through practices of exclusion, derision and bullying' (Epstein et al., 2003: 121). In particular, pathologized views of working-class children, their families and their local communities can 'nega-tively define urban young people's identities and engagements with schooling through notions of deficit and lack' (Archer et al., 2010: 50).

Recently, research in the UK, and elsewhere, has documented the way in which social class has continued to be implicated in educational achievement

(Ennals, 2004; Reay, 2006). Ball (2008: 173) claims that 'class differences and inequalities seem firmly entrenched and may even be getting worse'. As he has argued (Ball, 2003: 5), the actions of middle-class advantaged families work towards the 'perpetuation, inscription and reinvention of social inequalities both old and new'. In a market economy where (some) parents 'choose' their children's school, the evidence is that middle-class families, by and large, select schools with predominantly middle-class intakes, frequently in middle-class housing enclaves (Thrupp, 2007). Buying a house in the catchment area of a 'desirable' school can shore up privilege and ensure educational advantage. Thus, class, housing zones and middle-class cultural capital can and are deployed to bring off educational advantage (Kohn, 1998). Middle-class children predominantly attend middle-class schools that attract teachers who stay longer, access better resourcing and, recruit more pro-school students. These schools may also be less heterogeneous (in terms of 'race'/ethnic diversity); they certainly are in terms of socio-economic status. In cases like this, it seems unremarkable to talk of divided schools in divided cities. In educational terms, the issue is not about diversity in the city but is more about the avoidance of diversity, the marginalization of the 'other' and the reinforcement of widening gaps of inequalities; the reproduction of insiders and outsiders.

Activity

Talk to two very different people (older/younger; with/out children; un/waged; etc.) who live in the same neighbourhood.

Where do they shop? What transport do they use and why? Do they use any local resources such as the library, swimming pool, local park, etc. Where do they socialize? In what ways do these differences in their lived identities contribute to the ways in which they experience the neighbourhood?

Conclusion

In this chapter, we have designated the people of the city as being constituted as insiders and outsiders. We have argued that in some respects, the city offers a freedom and anonymity through which new identities can be constructed. The city offers some creative potential for making up multiple versions of the self, perhaps in relation to issues of gender, sexualities and desire. Nevertheless, there are specific contexts in which exclusions are clearly delineated, and class is one of these. The city is a place of difference and diversity; it is also marked by divisions. These come together to produce inequalities and exclusions, insiders and outsiders.

Further reading

Collins, A. (ed.) (2006) *Cities of Pleasure: Sex and the Urban Socialscape*. London and New York: Routledge.

Prakash, G. and Kruse, K. M. (eds) (2008) *The Spaces of the Modern City: Imaginaries, Politics, and Everyday Life*. Princeton and Oxford: Princeton University Press.

Toynbee, P. (2003) *Hard Work: Life in Low Pay Britain*. London: Bloomsbury.

Wood, P. and Landry, C. (2007) *The Intercultural City: Planning for Diversity Advantage*. London; Sterling, VA: Earthscan.

Useful websites

http://www.culf.org.uk
The Commission on Urban Life and faith
http://www.jrf.org.uk
Joseph Rowntree Foundation

The Virtual Urban

Introduction

This chapter takes a different approach towards theorizing the urban. It explores the urban physically and virtually in the light of the impact of technological change, particularly the internet. It explores opportunities as well as new divisions and inequalities and considers how technology can be both a promise and a problem to urban populations.

Castells (2002) has claimed that the emergence of the information society is the result of three developments: the social and cultural movements of the 1960s/1970s, the information technology 'revolution' in the 1970s and the restructuring of capitalism in the 1980s. As a consequence of these developments a new perspective of the city has emerged going beyond what Thrift (2000) has referred to as the traditional *city limit* of what cities used to be like in peoples' memories.

However, the information society has not resulted in the end of cities. Indeed, we are now living on an increasingly urbanized planet connected by global networks. Knowledge and information are now key currencies to generate wealth, jobs and power, and vibrant cities and metropolitan regions are the vital sources of such innovations. So modern city designers and planners have a number of challenges: they need to offer new and attractive place-based experiences that work with and complement the increasingly omnipresent internet; they need to support the emergence of 'hybrid space', that is the combining of urban space with electronic networks (Castells, 2001) and they need to respond to the fluidity of the 'anywhere, anytime' culture of ubiquitous technologies that are transforming the cities we live in (Greenfield, 2006). The issue in the transformed urban environment is not only about access to technologies or substituting virtual space for 'real' space. It is also about interaction and interdependence between the physical and the virtual: 'Sometimes we will use networks to avoid going places. But sometimes, still, we will go places to network' (Mitchell, 2000: 155). Therefore, those people who are in a position to take advantage of these spaces are further enabled to respond to the opportunities and choices presented by them.

Space and time

Technological advancements have changed peoples' relationships with space and time. Space is now less tied up with any particular place or locality. The emergence of the medium of computer-mediated communication has opened up a new sense of space through the creation of the 'virtual community' or 'cyber society'. An example of this is Virtuall.org (www.virtuall.org), the website name of the London Mental Health Learning Partnership learning and development initiative set up some time ago to link users, carers and frontline staff with the aim to improve mental health services across London (Hellawell, 2001). Using universal standardized time, people can interact at distance, away from physical environments and through face-to-face interactions as found in social networks such as Facebook and MySpace websites.

Giddens (1990; 2007) has claimed that society is witnessing an unprecedented level of continual change because of the acceleration of new technological and scientific innovations. The advance in technological developments and the emerging new social 'cyber'-structure go hand in hand. If one has access and resources, social relations are no longer tied to one place and

mediated through time. With the use of technology, communication tran-
scends physical and social constraints; there are potentially no borders or
barriers to any space–time distance. Information technologies can enable
greater interconnections between different people and organizations. For
example, Cyworld (www.cyworld.com), a South Korean virtual community
site launched in 1999, networks 90 per cent of young Korean people in their
late teens and early twenties (*Business Week*, 2005). Therefore we can
see traditional boundaries collapse. So, in essence, time and space become
compressed. This is particularly so for some in technologically advanced
societies, which have the scope to use and produce information technologies
to fuel and accelerate continual change. However, within this change there
is the potential to widen the gap between the 'haves' and the 'have nots', who
can become increasingly marginalized politically, economically and socially.

Giddens (1985) and Harvey (1989) argue that it is not only being excluded
that presents issues of concern about sustainable identities and communities.
Changing relationships between space and time have, to all intents and purposes, changed society. One outcome can be that there are greater difficulties
in forming strong social relationships because of a rise in physical isolation. As
early as 1977, Castells claimed that populations and spatial locales would
become more divided, fragmented and polarized because of technological
advances. Therefore, these issues are of particular significance for urban
education, the urban educator and for those people educated in urban
communities that are operating within an accelerating dialectic of change
and innovation.

Changing cities

In some ways the material city is shaped, ordered and delineated by specific
planning, requirements and functions, as the Chicago School of Sociologists
attempted to demonstrate in the 1920s. However, in other ways urban spaces
are not rational and ordered, but are non-linear, random, develop over time
and are changed by the movement of people.

Moreover, this particular geographical, physical model is being further
disrupted as people have become more electronically connected. A new form
of society is emerging, as argued by Van Dijk in *The Network Society* (1991).
In the *Rise of the Network Society*, Castells (1996) suggests that for some the
traditional city is being replaced by a new public realm, based around the

formation of electronic networks. Rather than being bounded by physical forms, these networks provide a social and economic structuring of their own, thereby creating the Network Society. Restructuring takes place in a global dimension because of the dynamic nature of networks and information flows. In practice, this has the potential to challenge the dominance of the bounded, physical city.

One substantive feature of the changing city is that because of the growth of information and communication technology (ICT), people are connected together in different and more complex ways. Castells identifies three key components of these connections: 'Linkages between activities, networks made up of organisations, and flows of production factors and of commodities' (1999: 47). These links enacted in cyberspace can mirror and extend the networks of everyday life, so for instance, we find 'a network of network cities' (Castells, 2001: 209). As a consequence of these networks, real cities are virtually connected and networked in real time. This means that people can be connected over greater areas in individual cities and between different cities, so that the social and spatial organization of the city and how people are connected in cities is challenged and will change (Mitchell, 1995).

Even more than with geographical space, the structure and geography of the virtual city (also known as the electronic, digital and cyber city) is characterized by unplanned, spontaneous and disordered activities. However, as Mitchell (1995) highlights, it will be the connectedness of these virtual spaces to real spaces that will be a determinant of the success of these emerging networks.

There are different types of virtual cities that range from those that are comparable to 'real' cities, through their capacity to create a 'real' sense of urban social life online, to less sophisticated and commercially driven web-based city listings or maps that provide an interface to electronic information about a city via the internet (Dodge et al., 1997). Although we can identify differences in conceptual processes, economic and material forms, lived practices and the geography of the virtual city, these are not dissimilar to the functioning and development of urban life, street systems and public places in 'real' cities. The virtual world Second Life (www.secondlife.com) provides an example of the emulation of physical space in the virtual. However, it is always worth noting that these virtual spaces are not merely representations of the physical and are only bounded by the limits of creativity and imagination.

The idea of moving between the spaces of the digitalized cyber city and the material city to produce a mixed reality of a more complex and hybrid urban life is becoming possible. The socio-geography and architecture of the cyber city may 'mirror' or replicate that of the physical city using satellite images, maps and three-dimensional buildings, as with Google Earth (www.earth. google.co.uk), so the experience can seem tangible and real. For example, Digital Urban, based at the Centre for Advanced Spatial Analysis at University College London, has modelled virtual urban environments to examine urban growth over time. These simulations allow people to experience a city environment that could previously only have been imagined. However, while virtual space design may be shaped by buildings and places found in the physical world, it is noteworthy that the plots of land being purchased in Second Life tend to be islands or parks – waterfronts with beaches and groves, a far cry from the urban spaces most people live in. Therefore, we can see here a tension that has previously existed for city dwellers of the idealized rural setting into the idealized virtual setting.

Most recently in the field of computer research, there has been resurgence in the importance of the physical with the development of Augmented Reality (AR). AR allows the perception of reality to be augmented or modified. In essence, real objects react to information streams to which they become sensitive, such as people and the environment. AR specifically generates composite views using the real scene viewed by the user and a virtual scene generated by the computer. The key aspect of AR is that the virtual elements enhance the person's performance and perception of the world by supplying relevant information that is *not* contained in the material world (Smith, 2009). There have been a number of mobile AR browsers recently developed which allow users to look at reality through the camera on their mobile phone with real-time digital information 'layered' on top, as has been trialled in Amsterdam (http://layar.com/). This is particularly valuable as it enables the individual to negotiate and have greater control of unfamiliar urban space via access to expert systems and social networks.

Activity

To what extent has identity of the city changed with the emergence of the internet? Think of some examples to support these views.

Defining and redefining urban community

This part will critically explore the changing nature of community that results from the emergence of online existence and virtual communities (Palloff and Pratt, 1999; Kenyon, 2006). Communities can be: 'Far-flung, loosely-bounded, sparsely-knit and fragmentary. Most people operate in multiple, thinly-connected, partial communities as they deal with networks of kin, neighbors, friends, workmates and organisational ties' (Wellman, 2001: 227).

Traditionally, membership of communities has tended to be place-based, where people lived and maintained their local connections. In many societies, traditional forms of association still persist. However, as the shift in community began with the move from rural to urban living as land-use patterns changed over periods of time, so in technologically advanced societies, where we live is becoming less important in terms of constructing our social groups. Building communities does not require people to gather in one place – more important is shared culture and practices.

The most remote locations across the globe can now be part of the information flows. New kinds of ties and support networks can be developed. These can have global concerns, such as climate change and sustainability as well as local urban issues. It is possible for small-scale initiatives in urban communities to take place and to be enhanced by the use of technology in order to improve communications and activities beyond the usual spatial constraints (Nunes, 2006). For example, within social care there are models where service users can come together to form groups outside of the formal institutionalized organizations and some have developed formal partnerships with health organizations. (Hellawell, 2001).

Higher levels of mobility may also result in people experiencing a reduced sense of localized community, giving rise to what Wellman refers to as 'personalized communities' (2001). Serra (2000) believes that these transformations particularly affect urban areas, breaking bonds that have traditionally held urban society together. Place-based, face-to-face activities are now removed or at least fragmented, allegedly resulting in weaker social ties, social isolation and an erosion of community (Nie and Erdring, 2000). However, Castells warns against following a simplistic dichotomy of

> The ideological opposition between the harmonious local community of an idealized past and the alienated existence of the lonely netizen, too often associated in the public image with the stereotype of a computer nerd. (2001: 117)

Some theorists claim that shifts away from traditional place-based communities may provide options and opportunities for new forms of communities through new spatial arrangements, based on needs and common interests created by online activity (Wellman, 2001; Castells, 2002). The key to the creation of these new forms of community, argue Graham and Aurigi (1997: 34), is that *virtual city life* needs to be grounded in, and remain connected to, lived experiences 'that draw the participants of interactions into meaningful, effective relationships with each other and with their city'.

Activity

Identify three different urban communities. Will technology strengthen these communities or weaken them?

Virtual communities

A virtual community is a group of individuals, groups of people, networks or the virtual public who 'interact around a shared interest, where the interaction is at least partially supported and/or mediated by technology and guided by some protocols or norms' (Porter, 2004: 4). To this extent then the global and local become interrelated in a networked social space. However, the location of the interaction among the community members, whether the purpose is social, commercial or professional, is in virtual rather than physical, geographical space and it can be either private or communal. This sense of space and sense of place is complex in terms of presence and location in virtual environments as well as how this relates to human interaction in the physical world (Castells, 2001). Indeed, Wellman claims that 'Although physical place continues to be important, cyberspace has become cyberplace, affecting the ways in which people find and maintain community' (2001: 247).

Traditionally the physical location was credited with bringing communities together. The internet is now able to do this on a global scale with the development of online communities, not just in terms of communication but in public networks of coordinated communities that Serra (2000) refers to as *intercommunities*. These are global, but also increasingly include local networks, that he refers to as a localnet service: 'The technology is global, but the people are local' (2000: 54). Furthermore, the networked local community can also go global and act globally – thereby replicating some aspects of location-based connectivity (Wellman, 1999). People can move between the global and local according to need at the click of a button. An example of the use of online networks linking to networked local and global communities is the Earth Day network (www.earthday.net). This is an initiative of the environmental movement, coordinated globally through the internet, which has concrete effects in the physical world in cities around the globe. For instance, Earth Day Network's Urban Environment Report (UER) scores the current performance of 72 US cities based on over 200 indicators of environmental, health, and social problems and measures the concentration of citizens who are most vulnerable (Selun, 2009). In this case technology is connecting the local to the global which allows for political action locally that has global consequences (also see Chapter 5).

The emergence of these virtual communities has raised debates about what 'community' actually means in terms of different social relationships and support for sociability (Castells, 2001). An example of this is provided by youth worker Gavin Sealey when setting up the virtual youth club NYPO: 'The way young people interact with me has changed – they've got the power. It's all about power and the internet is freeing up power from institutions' (cited in Hellawell, 2001: 37). As with any power shift there is going to be resistance, particularly when that shift is to *the people*.

Deliberations about the nature of connectivity reflect earlier urban socio-logical debates: about on the one hand how urbanization destroys meaningful community life that is replaced by weaker ties; and on the other hand how the city frees people from traditional forms of social control (Castells, 2001). These issues around connectivity and power have been explored in nineteenth- and twentieth-century literature, such as in the urban writings of Charles Dickens and Raymond Chandler that show the possibility of human agency and change. Whereas darker and more pessimistic works such as Huxley's *Brave New World* (1932) or Orwell's *Nineteen Eighty-Four* (1949) point to how societies can transmute into totalitarian regimes of invasive social control and surveillance, with people conditioned to lose their individual identities, when new tech-nologies are used without appropriate accountability.

So, it is necessary for us to extend our understanding of urban community and the part this plays in individual identity-making processes. Online, elec-tronic and virtual communities mirror urban environments (Burrows, 1997) and provide the opportunity to create new sorts of social relationships that also extend the opportunity of individual agency.

Some people still see the internet as place-based in a virtual sense rather than as a network (Shell, 1995) and as many people are in search of community this can be re-assuring. However, community is now not necessarily spatially or location-based. Many cities, such as Amsterdam, Bologna and Kyoto are now terming themselves 'digital cities' by providing a public technological infrastructure based on an urban metaphor, networking local communities and integrating information about everyday community life to support public participation in a variety of social activities. Another technological innovation has been the development of Arabiananta, a suburb of Helsinki in Finland, which claims to be the world's first virtual business and residential community (www.arabianranta.fi). As well as being a real-world community, it is planned that the whole area will have constant wireless interactive connectivity, known as the Helsinki Virtual Village. The limits that were created by both space and time in the material world will no longer constrain people's social worlds as information and services can be available electronically as an everyday part of peoples' lives (Aurigi, 2005). However, as with all social activity there are different ideologies being played out and issues of power and control need to be critically considered. As with the physical city, there is both public and (private) controlled access in cyberspace that can or cannot be traversed, at times creating contested divisions and hierarchies (Mitchell, 1995).

Cyberspace can operate in a similar way to everyday life, but offers the potential to plan encounters in multimedia environments that may not be possible in physical life (Wellman, 1999). In terms of educational applications, the appeal of using virtual worlds allows the participants to develop co-presence in real-time, simulated environments, so space is redefined away from the bricks and mortar of previous generations. One example of this is the use of the computer simulation game Sim City (www.simcity.ea.com), which involves participants in making decisions, for example about the environmental impact on the running of a city and its amenities by extending their analytical and critical skills.

Virtual worlds and virtual communities offer new educational experiences. There are applications in terms of blending real and virtual experiences into hybrids in educational contexts, such as in multimedia role plays and field trips. One real-life example is a multimedia game developed by Geese Theatre Company (www.geese.co.uk) called Lifting the Weight that has been used with young offenders in Feltham Young Offenders Institute in West London to help them stay out of trouble when they return to the community (Hellawell, 2001).

Another example is a virtual youth club and magazine, Newham Young People Online (www.nypo.org) that was set up in East London for young people (11–25 years) to enhance peer social networks and discuss a range of topical and sometimes controversial issues as well as chat online (Hellawell, 2001). This may help to build confidence and give voice in a platform that can be less intimidating than face-to-face communication and offer the potential for personal growth.

Online communities can be extended into communities of practice, where larger groups of people can share and develop expertise and good practice, participate in discussions and decision-making (Lave and Wenger, 1998). This can be seen as mirroring mass movements found in traditional urban settings attended by informed and concerned individuals and groups. However, online communities of practice tend to focus on single issues and draw upon the collective expertise to challenge institutions and power.

Virtual communities may also help to re-establish a sense of community in settings where people have retreated to residential enclaves. In some cases they may have only ventured beyond their gated communities in their cars, reducing the possibility of the chance encounter of face-to-face interactions that was a characteristic of the urban setting. Wellman (2001: 234) points out that 'Physical closeness does not mean social closeness'.

So although urban living is increasing, the potential for greater physical contact can be diminishing. This social isolation can be replicated online, resulting in the creation of new forms of isolation in front of the computer screen.

At a time when face-to-face social relationships and bonds may be diminishing (Burrows, 1997), cyberspace provides an opportunity for people to expand their circles of social contact beyond their vicinity. This could be referred to as 'a social technology' (Serra, 2000: 50). In essence, the internet has reordered the world into a network society and offered people a chance to gain a sense of global as well as local community-building.

Activity

How can virtual communities transform urban populations in ways that liberate and share power rather than promote more control?

The digital divide

In all this talk of the promise of new technologies and new online communities, it is easy to forget that there may be some structural and material obstacles in the networked society. The digital divide has become a generic term that refers to the gap between individuals, some sectors of communities, different countries or regions in terms of differences in access to ICTs. This divide penetrates into economic, social and educational life. Frequently, those who are not online are also disadvantaged in other ways (Livingstone et al., 2005). Internet access is an issue of economic and social access and the disparities of everyday life and the patterns of exclusion experienced in the physical world may be transferred to the virtual world. In the UK, it is evident that families from low-income backgrounds benefit least from internet access (Becta, 2008a; Helsper, 2008). Furthermore, those with greater economic and social capital and who are otherwise advantaged (Bourdieu, 2007), may be self-limiting by engaging in uncritical online activities rather than with the complexities that the urban context still offers.

There are many people around the world who are excluded from the Information Society. This may be due to lack of funds, central government initiatives, effective strategies for E-learning and inadequate human expertise. In March 2009, 81.5 per cent of the world internet users were in Asia, Europe and North America (http://www.internetworldstats.com/stats.htm). For those countries that were exploited by colonialism, now, if they do not have ICT infrastructure, they may well be seen as irrelevant or disadvantaged and open to further exploitation (Castells, 1999). Indeed, Castells claims that without an internet-based economy and management system, it is not possible for any country to generate the sustainable resources, whether economic, social or environmental, necessary to support its needs (Castells, 2001). This is part of the many arguments for closing the international digital divide in terms of economic and social equality, economic growth and democracy.

Uneven developments in urban living and lifestyles as cities have become globalized and digitalized have resulted in a lack of access among those living in the most disadvantaged and deprived areas. 'The inclusionary rhetoric of the "information superhighway" seems somewhat hollow' (Graham and Aurigi, 1997: 24). What is occurring is an increasing gap between connected and unconnected populations that deepens the divide (Serra, 2000).

Graham and Aurigi (1997) refer to three groups: the information users, the information used and the information excluded, and they ask whether virtual cities can really help restore 'The disfigured city, the offline spaces and electronic ghettos of decay, poverty, and exclusion, where few have the resources to go on-line?' (p. 35). This imbalance is because greater use of the internet occurs in those areas where there are concentrations of the information economy. Unequal access for certain minority groups and low-income households, reductions in price of hardware and greater range of methods to go online are starting to address this barrier (Castells, 2001). In the UK context, the government has set up initiatives such as UK online centres (www.ukonlinecentres.com) and learndirect centres (www.learndirect.co.uk) in public venues such as libraries and cyber-cafes, often located in city areas of greatest inequality and deprivation (Strategy Unit, 2005). Although these may not be equitable, for instance due to limited access and availability, they may ameliorate the effects of the digital divide.

Activity

Carry out an informal audit in an urban setting of public services that give access to online resources. To what extent do they meet the needs of the local community?

Conclusion

It could be argued that the idea of the virtual urban has an air of science fiction to it. However, in the twenty-first century, the use of ICT is rapidly changing society. As a result, key elements of urban space and communities, how we live, work, learn and play will become affected and shaped or reshaped because of technologies.

Therefore the notions of location and place, previously significant to any discussion about the urban (Saunders, 1981), is for some less relevant now and for others multifaceted. Certainly cities are changing as a result of technologies, as the physical, material and virtual worlds are developing together in more complex ways.

Technologies have the potential to provide people with a wealth of opportunities and benefits that may not be possible in the material world. New communities are formed which can enhance traditional, existing communities but also change them for the better.

The digital divide exists in many contexts. However, people who are economically disadvantaged and socially isolated are often to be found in urban settings. Therefore, social exclusion will often mirror digital exclusion. People need to possess social and cultural capital, as well as economic capital, in order to take advantage of technological advancements. It is not only access to technologies that divides people, although cost is still a barrier (Becta, 2008a). The problem also involves economic, cultural and social factors, concerning how and to what extent, those previously disenfranchised, can engage with technologies usefully, in order to make a difference and enable them to live better lives.

Further reading

Castells, M. (1996) *The Rise of the Network Society*. London: Blackwell.

Sheller, M. and Urry, J. (eds) (2006) *Mobile Technologies of the City*. London: Routledge.

Useful websites

http://www.communities.gov.uk/publications/communities/technologyfutures

Communities and Local Government (2008), Technology Futures and Digital Inclusion – Research Report. London: Crown

http://www.sleducation.wikispaces.com

Second Life in Education

Part 2
Urban Education in Changing Times

In this second part, we turn more directly to some of the themes that are typical of the field of urban education studies and schooling. In a concern to take seriously our topic of 'change', we explore the influence of neo-liberal economics and global–local imperatives as they play out in urban education settings. Urban settings are places of fluidity, diversity and difference. Thus, in these changing times, policy decisions have to be made about which aspects of 'difference' and change should be reflected in the educational system in order to maintain a socially just, yet socially cohesive, society. In this section we explore these themes in respect of the provision of faith schools in the UK. We also consider the continuities that have patterned policy-making in response to urban schools and ask if these sorts of responses are still fit for changing times.

Culture, Faith and Community

Introduction

This chapter explores some of the complexities related to cultural diversity and social justice in urban settings in the provision of faith schools. 'Discussions, dialogues and debates on the role of faith schools, and their effect on community cohesion often create more heat than light . . . and the debate still rages today' (Berkeley, 2008).

What we intend to do in this chapter is to explore the various claims for and against the recognition of faith as an aspect of diversity and identity within state educational provision. At the centre of this debate are concerns about social cohesion, issues of difference, respect and recognition, as well as community rights and responsibilities in an increasingly diverse, urbanized society. Currently in the UK, over one-third of all state-maintained schools are faith schools and many have a long history of providing education (Berkeley, 2008). However, in an increasingly secularized society, are faith schools a vehicle for cohesion or are they socially divisive?

Faith and diversity in the urban setting

New arrivals to the UK have tended to settle in cities where the likelihood of affordable housing and work has been more available. Frequently, settlements have expanded in places where the arriving communities have already started to establish and maintain 'meeting centres, supplementary schools and places of worship' (Maguire, Wooldridge and Pratt-Adams, 2006: 87). For example, studies of the East End of London in the nineteenth century have illustrated the ways in which various communities settled over time, establishing schools and places of worship and then gradually moved out as they were able to access better housing and other opportunities (Fishman, 1988). This pattern of movement is illustrated in the ways that places of worship have changed their denominational character over time. In the East End, Anglican Churches were taken over by French Huguenots, then re-designated as Synagogues and more recently some have been transformed into Mosques (Kershen, 2005). The current Brick Lane Mosque was formerly the Machzike Adass Synagogue – Spitalfield's Great Synagogue and before that a Huguenot meeting house. Traces of the settlement patterns of various faith communities are etched into the urban fabric in this way across many of the major cities of the UK.

Currently, even though housing patterns are far less homogenous than they were in the nineteenth century, the intake of many urban schools in the twenty-first century still reflects and mirrors older patterns of settlement. Thus, in parts of many cities, housing occupancy and school intakes reflect the local patterns of settlement and local histories of employment over time as well as in terms of more recent arrivals (Belchem, 2007). A key factor in characterizing culturally diverse urban schools is that they still predominantly serve working-class communities who have settled and are housed in these areas (Lupton, 2004). Additionally, many of the urban dwellers who are caught up in poverty are members of minority groups who may also have different religious and cultural heritages. In sum, 'the issue of diversity is fundamental to the demography and the experience of the city' (Stevenson,

2003: 51) and has always been and remains one of the dimensions of this phenomenon.

In the recent past, issues of diversity have been raised because of concerns about inequality between different communities and constituencies and policies have attempted to ameliorate reduced access to social and material goods such as housing, education and health provision. More recently, with the move towards a culturalist analysis of the city (Fincher and Jacobs, 1998), concerns have moved onto issues of difference and how these are being mediated, recognized and reflected (or not) in state welfare provision. Urban cultures are characterized by diversities and complex intersectionalities of identities, histories and contemporary experiences. Older categorizations of identity based solely on attributes of 'race', class or gender may not always do justice to the complexities of what Bondi (1993) has called the 'hyphenated identities' that most people inhabit – such as 'white-Jewish-woman'. However, the dimension of faith and its part in shaping the lived identities of urban dwellers has been under-researched in the urban education literature (but see Archer, 2003). Thus, in this chapter we want to take seriously the ways in which, while it is

> possible for some people to have a number of social identities . . . there may be a religious rather than an ethnic boundary . . . a marker which helps to define their sense of who they are, and helps reinforce the strength of their religious belief. (Parker-Jenkins et al., 2005: 5)

One question that needs to be posed is this: Does taking faith identity seriously and respectfully involve the need to provide state maintained faith schools?

Faith schools, identity and community

In exploring the complexities involved in setting up and maintaining faith schools in the UK, two points need to be considered. First, some groups may see faith schools as fundamental in supporting their identity and maintaining, defending and preserving their community (Valins, 2003). The second aspect concerns shifts over time that change identities within communities; from being settlers to becoming citizens, as well as changes within faith communities themselves (Modood, 1997). Thus, the expectations of schooling (faith and/or secular) may be constructed differently over time within various communities.

Many communities have regarded the provision of faith schools as a key part in maintaining the core of their cultural identity. Valins (2003: 235) says of Jewish schools that 'many Jewish leaders see these institutions as crucial to "fixing" children's religious, social and cultural identities'. He goes on to say that while these schools and these sentiments may be seen as 'exclusionary', they can also be seen as 'key to preserving a community at major risk from demographic decline and fragmentation' (2003: 236). Many other faith communities would probably share these views to some degree, although it could be argued that attempts to 'fix' identities in this way could be a form of denying childrens' human rights. Communities that initially fled to the UK to escape forms of persecution, poverty or other types of exclusion initially set up 'their' own schools in order to offer succour to the newly arrived and frequently dispossessed families. These communities have experienced a history of a long and hard struggle to obtain state funding and legal recognition of their rights to their own schools. Many faith-based schools were set up and are still being set up after a long struggle for equal treatment (compared with the 'established' Church of England schools, and then Roman Catholic and Jewish schools), in a context of maintaining their religious identity in periods of sometimes overt and hostile discrimination (Weller, 2006). In situations like this, faith schooling can sometimes provide a haven and a place of safety.

In any discussion of faith communities, it is important to acknowledge complexities and changes within and surrounding these groups. Many of the older and longer established faith communities in the UK, such as the Roman Catholic and Jewish constituencies, have changed significantly over time. For example, while the first Roman Catholic settlers in the UK came from Ireland and were predominantly of rural, working-class backgrounds, currently the UK Catholic community is far more heterogeneous. Families from many Latin American communities, from South Asia and the Philippines as well as from other historically Catholic European nations such as Poland have settled in the UK. Communities shift over time and with relationships forming between people from different (or no) faith backgrounds, the boundaries around faith groups have become more diffuse. As long ago as 1994, for example, the Chief Rabbi Jonathan Sacks was warning that 'young Jews are disengaging, disaffiliating and drifting away from Judaism' (cited in Valins, 2003: 240). Many of the members of these older, established faith communities are now third-and sometimes fourth-generation British citizens who share the same rights as all other citizens and assert their right to funding for faith-based schools. Another point of distinction relates to differences within these communities. These may include differences in interpretation of faith and orthodoxies as well as cultural and social beliefs and values. These differences may be seen, for example, in the various schools of thought within Islam and communities formed by different Rabbis within Judaism.

In the UK, many faith communities initially set up schools outside the state-maintained sector in order to support their children through teaching about their history, traditions, language and religion (Rutter, 1998). In some cases, these schools were a prelude to full inclusion and full funding by the state (Grace, 2001). Other supplementary schools have had a different mission entirely. One view has been that supplementary schools have had to do just that – supplement the gaps in what is provided by state schooling for children from minoritized backgrounds. A stronger perspective has argued that some of these schools may be better regarded as new social movements; schools that are working with communities to provide a more radical form of education, organized and led by local groups (Safia-Mirza and Reay, 2000). Although these supplementary schools are important and make a powerful contribution (see Strand, 2007), in this chapter we want to focus specifically on faith schools within the state-maintained sector. For when it comes to decisions about what the state should or should not fund in relation to issues of community, faith and culture, there is a central tension between respect for 'diversity' and the need for social cohesion that is played out in the public policy arena. As Judge (2001: 463) has claimed:

> The arrangements currently in force in various parts of Britain are the result of complex historical compromises and any further extension of state aid to faith-based schools is likely to lead to an unwelcome fragmentation of society and a diversion of resources from schools committed to developing a common culture, while respecting a diversity of cultural identities.

Faith schools, which is those schools funded by the state that provide an education for children and students in a context of a specific religion or faith, have a long, complex and changing history in the UK. For example, in 2001, the New Labour White Paper *Schools: Building on Success* (DfES, 2001) was supportive of the Church of England's plans to establish 100 new schools and was supportive of faith schools more generally. More recently, there has been a pulling back from this position. 'It is up to the local community to decide what it wants. We are not leading a drive for more faith schools' (House of Commons Children, Schools and Families Select Committee, 2008). However, currently more than one-third of state schools in England have a 'religious character' (Berkeley, 2008). While the majority are Church of England and Roman Catholic, there are also Jewish, Muslim, Hindu, Sikh and a small number of 'other Christian schools'.

Activity

To what extent do faith schools promote choice and/or provide a 'lifeline to and for these religious groups', a lifeline that 'connects children and parents to their historical and cultural religious groups'? (McKinney, 2008: 113)
Should the state be providing denominational schools?

From equality of opportunity to social justice

One of the justifications for the provision of faith schools rests on claims about the right to equality of treatment. If there are Church of England, Roman Catholic and Jewish schools, then there ought to be schools for other faith groups. While equality claims such as these do have some currency, they do not help in coming to decisions about more complex matters such as which faith groups should not be state supported in providing schooling. Recently, and in part because of the recognition of limits in equality of opportunity discourses, attention has turned towards considering the ways in which education can promote social justice. Social justice as it is conceived by Fraser (1997) has three elements – a distributive element; that is, a concern with ensuring that goods (material and otherwise) are distributed in a just manner. There is a cultural dimension that involves recognition and respect for differences. Associational forms of justice relate to the need to ensure that those who are excluded become included in decision-making activities. As Cribb and Gewirtz (2003: 19) explain, 'for distributive and cultural justice to be achieved it is necessary for previously subordinated groups to participate fully in decisions about how the principles of distribution and recognition should be defined and implemented'.

Cribb and Gewirtz add that this process of associational justice may be 'far from straightforward in practice' (2003: 19) given the many and complex long-standing forms of exclusion and injustices that these groups may well have experienced. For reasons partly based on the dimension of associational justice, the 'stronger' versions of supplementary schools as social movements have been founded in many urban centres.

Activity

What forms of social justice are evident in calls for faith-based schooling?

What (if any) tensions exist between these different forms in relation to the provision of faith schooling?

There is one more issue in understanding social justice and how to achieve it. As Gewirtz (2006: 70) makes clear, 'it is not possible to resolve the question of what counts as justice in education at a purely abstract level'. Her case is that justice 'can only properly be understood within specific contexts of interpretation'. Justice is multidimensional and thus, there may be tensions between different forms. So, recognizing the need for faith schools in terms of distributional justice and providing more faith schools of different denominations may marginalize other forms of cultural recognition in educational provision such as secularism or humanism. In terms of making decisions about how to act, there may also be tensions in terms of competing social justice issues between the claims of different groups; for example, between the Anglican community and Scientologists (who have not gained legal permission to set up schools). Gewirtz argues that 'in the real world principles do not translate directly into practice – there can only be partial degrees of success' (p. 90). She also points out that there can be other problems in terms of dealing with differences. Taking difference seriously does not mean that all differences are equally worthwhile or worthy of consideration. Coming to decisions about education policy and practice through privileging the views of parents, clerics and religious groups may seriously erode the human rights of children whose rights become 'secondary to the rights and interests of parents' (Kassen and Murphy, 2009: 78). Faith schools may, it is argued, limit the freedom of children to develop as an 'autonomous individual free from the shackles of indoctrination' (Kassen and Murphy, 2009: 79).

Social justice and faith communities

From what we have been arguing, it would seem that claims from within non-established faith communities for their own schools could be seen as socially just, particularly in the UK setting. Some faith groups have historically been able to have schools that reflected their faith perspectives in terms of aspects of the curriculum (particularly religious education), staffing profiles (head teachers of the same religious group) and shared community experiences (assembly and prayer). Thus, it is hard to see why this right should not be extended to other faith groups. This could be seen as fair in terms of distributive justice, cultural justice and associational forms of justice.

Parker-Jenkins et al. (2005: 183) report that some faith communities regard a multi-faith approach as 'inadequate, failing to provide for the spiritual and moral development of children'. They also suggest that 'the government's decision to expand faith-based schools can be seen as a victory for parental choice' (p. 182). Thus, cultural forms of social justice as recognition are being provided through the establishment of faith schools. This provision raises questions about whose rights are being supported by the state funding of faith schools (parents or children) and the extent to which the child has any voice or choice in this matter, as we have already signalled. However, as Lawton and Cairns (2005: 247) point out, 'not all parents in faith communities choose to send any or all of their children to a faith school'; school choice may be more to do with the 'needs and personality of each child' rather than anything to do with faith-identity.

There are also social justice issues related to questions around what is a community and who speaks for this group. Currently in Britain, many changes are taking place within and between different communities. The ways in which 'communities' are formed, shift and become reworked over time also needs to be recognized. Indeed, the concept of 'community' itself will mean different things to different groups. Some communities may almost be 'invisible' while others may be more actively engaged in retaining their heritage and 'trying to secure toleration of difference from the wider society' (Parker-Jenkins et al., 2005: 68). Communities and cultures change over time. They are frequently diverse and typically intersected by differences of place of origin, community language, class and gender, as well as generational differences, although they may mobilize at strategically critical moments (Benton and Gomez, 2007). One example of this complexity could be illustrated by the heterogeneity within the many different British Muslim communities. Then there are also tensions within many faith communities over human rights issues and sexualities and the rights of women, for example. In consequence, there are social justice questions related to who speaks for, and who claims to represent 'the community' in terms of education (and other matters).

Activity

Are the rights of some faith communities more protected than those of others that may be viewed as less socially acceptable? What about the rights of secularized communities?

Faith schools – cohesive or divisive?

The main point of tension that arises in relation to the calls for state-funded faith schools centres around questions about the sort of society that is desirable for the UK in the twenty-first century (McKinney, 2008). Are faith schools divisive? Are they oppressive? Can faith schools help to promote social cohesion or, by existing, do they render cohesion harder to achieve (Osler, 2007)? In respecting the wishes of certain faith groups, are we in danger of reducing the choices and rights of other groups in society as well as the choices and rights of those within the faith group itself? Are we in danger of 'ghettoizing' our children in school?

In a report for the Runnymede Trust, Berkeley (2008: 4) argues that schools 'are crucial in breaking down barriers between young people'. Against an international background of the attacks of 11 September 2001 in New York and the London bombings of 7 July 2005, 'issues of citizenship, national identity and belonging' (Osler, 2007: 5) have been foregrounded in Government concerns that schools promote community cohesion (DCSF, 2007a). Additionally, as a consequence of the urban 'disturbances' in Bradford, Burnley and Oldham in 2001 that were based on tensions between different (ethnic, cultural and religious) communities, two reports (Ousley, 2001; Cantle Team Review, 2001) into the causes and remedies for these outbreaks of violence and antagonism came to similar conclusions. They found that a 'virtual apartheid' in schools had failed to promote understanding of and respect for diversity and difference. Indeed, many urban communities who lived side by side in the same locations, sometimes in the same streets, did so without any apparent links or shared experiences. Children were not being educated together and thus the communities lived almost 'parallel lives' without contact, little understanding of one another or any significant shared experiences. Thus, the Runnymede Trust has concluded that faith schools, if they are to continue as part of the state-maintained sector, should accept a much broader intake of children from diverse backgrounds in order to promote cohesion, mutual recognition and understanding: 'As currently constituted they (faith schools) may be having the effect of limiting young people's ability to engage in such discussions' (Berkeley, 2008: 5). However, this does beg the question whether it is the faith per se that does the 'limiting' or it is an aspect of the in-school pedagogy. It begs a second question; do some faith schools have more oppressive practices than others?

Many of the teacher unions are similarly concerned about the issue of faith schools in terms of social cohesion (Association of Teachers and Lecturers, ATL, 2007; National Union of Teachers, NUT, 2008). For example, the ATL (2007) say that the UK Government has a commitment to faith schools as they are 'perceived' to be good at delivering higher achievement in examinations. They are popular with parents because of their academic 'success' and their alleged capability in providing 'coherent morality systems for pupils' (ATL, 2007: 1). The ATL add a note of caution; 'as the evidence on whether current faith schools actually deliver these objectives is mixed, it is highly questionable that their expansion will do so' (ATL, 2007: 1).

A pilot study conducted by West et al. (2007) found that Church of England schools tended to be more inclusive than other faith schools. The three Jewish schools in their sample only had children on roll who were reported to be Jewish. The Roman Catholic schools were predominantly Christian, with nine out of ten children who were enrolled being described in this way. The Church of England schools in the pilot study were, overall, more inclusive. On average, seven out of ten children were identified as Christian, one out of ten as Muslim. The researchers concluded that if social cohesion was to be taken more seriously then schools of a 'religious character' needed to be inclusive of all religions and of those of no faith. They concluded that 'given that public money is used to fund schools with a religious character there is a strong case to be made for such schools to be open to the wider community in the interests of enhancing social cohesion' (West et al., 2007).

Osler (2007) conducted research in six different urban locations in the UK with local stakeholders in order to explore issues related to faith schools.

Some of the questions that she raised drew attention to local factors involved in school choice. Different areas presented stark differences in the provision of faith schools or non-faith schools. Some areas had Islamic schools; others only had Christian schools. Locality made a significant difference to choosing schools. Osler also found what she called 'an obvious point to make' but something that is not always factored into these sorts of discussions: 'not all people of faith are advocates of faith-based education'. Similarly, Sullivan (2000: 16) has argued, for example, that Roman Catholic schools 'should never be seen as something ultimate or of supreme and unquestioned value'. He argues that there may be different needs and what he calls 'alternative approaches to Christian formation and to the Church's influence on education'. However, as Osler found, even though faith schools were seen as 'good' in many areas, they were not always seen as 'good' in terms of their spiritual dimension, but tended to be valued for their good results. Not surprisingly, Osler (2007: 7) found, 'faith schooling may also have a class dimension'. Thus, there may be forms of exclusion at work in the selection processes for some of the more academically successful faith schools.

West et al. (2007) found in their survey of admissions policies and practices in faith-based Secondary Schools in London that more than half of the 44 schools surveyed asked prospective parents to complete supplementary admissions forms. These schools required a testimonial from a minister or religious leader to confirm that the family were practising members of that faith. Those faith schools that were deliberately more inclusive retained a proportion of places for students of different and no faith backgrounds. As with Osler's research, West et al. (2007) found that 'Schools that were inclusive of other religions were not necessarily inclusive in other respects. In particular, an analysis of admissions criteria and supplementary admissions forms used suggested that, in some cases, they offered schools opportunities for social selection'.

For reasons of alleged 'selection by the back door' as well as concerns about social cohesion, the Runnymede Trust (Berkeley, 2008) has argued that faith schools should end selection based on faith and recruit a more inclusive intake. As they state, 'if faith schools are convinced of their relevance for society, then that should apply equally for all children' (Berkeley, 2008: 3). The same report calls for faith schools to serve 'the most disadvantaged':

> Despite histories based on challenging poverty and inequality, and high-level pronouncements that suggest a mission to serve the most disadvantaged in

society, faith schools educate a disproportionately small number of young people at the lowest end of the socio-economic scale. (Berkeley, 2008: 3)

The report does not call for an end for faith schools; it does call for these schools to 'become schools for all'.

Conclusion

Overall, then, there are a number of questions that are connected to culture, faith and community in urban educational provision. One of these concerns the role that faith schools play in society. Kassem and Murphy (2009: 79) argue that: 'The policy of faith schools is in fact creating a segregated system that does little to address the agenda towards social inclusion, but instead opens a gaping chasm of social and economic division based on social class'.

There are strong arguments for the preservation and expansion of faith-based schools, where demand exists, in terms of distributive social justice and as a marker of recognition and respect. There are also questions related to associational forms of justice in questioning who decides about the provision (or not) of faith schools. However, faith is only one dimension of identity and other aspects related to class, gender, age, sexualities, aptitude and ethnicity, for instance, all need careful consideration. 'It is not enough to privilege one marker of identity over all others' (Berkeley, 2008: 6). Currently, there seems to be some acceptance of the fairness in providing new faith schools given the existence of many others in the state-maintained sector (Parker-Jenkins et al., 2005; Berkeley, 2008). However, research that has explored these schools suggests that their intakes are somewhat skewed:

DfES figures for England in 2005 have shown that in the average community primary school 20.1 percent of children are eligible for free school meals. In the average Church of England primary it is only 11.3 per cent. Similarly, around 15.4 per cent of students in community secondaries are eligible for free school meals, whilst in faith-based secondaries this drops to an average of 11.6 per cent. (NUT, 2008: 19)

There are critics of faith-based schools who argue that these schools are socially divisive and do little to ensure social inclusion and cohesion. One suggestion is that it is now time to move away from the traditional historical settlement of faith schooling being supported by the state.

. . . the only non-racist route is to remove religion from all functions of the state . . . instead the government is digging a bigger hole, storing up worse trouble for the future, as atheist white middle-classes demand more (selective) church schools while Muslims choose segregation too. (Toynbee 2001, cited in Parker-Jenkins et al., 2005: 181)

In terms of public policy and faith schools, it seems unlikely that these schools will be closed down. As Parker-Jenkins et al. (2005: 203) argue, 'good schools are popular and poor schools are not, regardless of whether they have a religious character'. In producing an inclusive education for all, what is needed, they suggest, is needed, they suggest, for all schools to 'demonstrate an active commitment to social justice and make a positive contribution to the pursuit of social harmony'. Perhaps the key question is the degree to which this is possible in the current state school system.

Pring (2005: 56) argues that the debate about faith schools should include a discussion of the aims and intentions of education, 'its underlying notions of rationality, the significance attached to autonomy and the concern over indoctrination'. Is it the role of education to support faith or is it the job of schools to enable young people to 'engage in an informed, sensitive and intelligent manner with questions about the ultimate meaning and purpose of life' (Brandom, et al., 2007: 290)? It has not been possible in this short chapter to give due attention to these questions that do have to be addressed if faith schools are to maintain what Pring (2005: 60) refers to as 'their precarious hold on public support'. This is particularly the case in the light of claims about selection and social exclusion in faith schools. In addition, Lawton and Cairns (2005) believe that democratic states have to guard against illiberalism and intolerance in trying to promote social justice. It is not simply the case that any group that positions itself as a faith community should have the right to set up schools on the basis of claims about distributive justice – other aspects have to be considered, such as respect and tolerance for difference as well as not creating or perpetrating internal apartheids and injustices within the faith group itself because of the provision of faith schools.

In the schools of the inner cities, in settings of cosmopolitan diversity, children and young people of many faiths and no faiths will be growing up in close proximity to one another. The current situation is that many of the state-supported faith schools that serve these communities do not always respond positively to calls to enhance inclusion, social justice and social cohesion. These faith-based schools may be part of the problem rather than being part of the solution, sometimes in a way that 'contradicts the moral teachings of the faiths themselves' through perpetuating discrimination and exclusion (Pring, 2005: 60). However, Halstead and McLaughlin (2005: 71) argue that other types of schools may be similarly divisive and that any 'unfair privilege' involved in attending faith-based schools could be dealt with by 'equalising provision and resources, rather than getting rid of the whole category of faith schools'.

At the heart of this issue about how urban education should respond to culture, faith and difference in relation to faith schools is a struggle over competing claims about rights, recognition and needs. These are set against questions about the role of the state in providing support for some aspects of some cultures in the school system. These debates may be more acute in urban settings, where many parents, for diverse reasons, continue to seek out and select faith-based schools for their children. However, there are other views that have not been foregrounded in this chapter but which also need to be considered. The views of secularists and of those with strong commitments towards equal rights might oppose the maintenance of faith schools by the state, particularly those schools that they may see as oppressive in terms of gender or sexuality. Thus, if faith schools are to continue to be state funded, then at the very least 'we should demand their commitment to the wider community, and a demonstration of socially just educational practices' (Parker-Jenkins et al., 2005: 202).

Further reading

Cairns, J. (2009) *Faith Schools, and Society: Civilizing the Debate*. London: Continuum.

Coles, M. I. (2008) *Every Muslim Child Matters: Practical Guidance for Schools and Children's Services*. Oakhill, VA: Trentham.

Maguire, M. and Pratt-Adams, S. (2009) 'Urban education, equality and inequality', in Hill, D. and Helavaara Robertson, L. (eds) *Equality in the Primary School*. London: Continuum International Publishers.

Odone, C. (2008) *In Bad Faith: The New Betrayal of Faith Schools*. London: Centre for Policy Studies.

Useful websites

http://www.runnymedetrust.org/
The Runnymede Trust
http://www.teachernet.gov.uk/wholeschool/faithschools/
Teachernet

Urban Education in a Global Context

5

Chapter Outline

Introduction

This chapter will analyse the impact of globalization on urban education. It will begin by offering an explanation of the process of globalization. The chapter will then consider the interconnectivity, integration and interdependence of different nations, with a particular focus on the socio-economic aspect of globalization. Gottdiener and Hutchison (2006) claim that the global world is also the urban world, so the chapter will also explore how globalization has impacted on the notion of urban community. The chapter will consider the uneven development in cities as a consequence of globalization. Following this, the impact of globalization on urban education will be explored. The final section presents examples of 'glocal' initiatives addressing urban education.

The process of globalization

Colonialism, military imperialism and the domination and exploitation of one society by another have a long history as evidenced by the ancient civilizations of China, Greece and Rome. So, in some ways it could be claimed that globalization is not a new phenomenon, even if the term is most frequently employed to denote recent developments. In the nineteenth century there was already a global trade economy. The European colonial nations forged connections and established cities such as Lagos and Sao Paulo. Raw materials were brought across the globe to be traded in European cities to support expanding economies. In fact, many influences of former colonial times still remain and the networks created by globalization are often viewed as legacies of a neo-colonial process that began centuries before (Carroll-Miranda, 2006). During the Industrial period of the nineteenth century, cities such as Manchester, Frankfurt and Chicago became centres of industrial and commercial activity. However, it has been claimed that present-day globalization is distinct from past hierarchies that were controlled and dependent on an 'imperial centre' (Spybey, 2001; Cohen and Kennedy, 2007), as we shall see.

It has been claimed that it is difficult to define and comprehend globalization (Giddens, 1999; Lauder et al., 2006). The concept and process of globalization is a condensate made up from the following aspects:

- An increase in commercial networks of powerful trans-national organizations;
- alleged diminishing national boundaries, greater international linkage and inter-dependence of peoples and increases in cultural interactions;
- restructuring of time and space – the acceleration of the experience of time and reduction in the significance of distance and spatial arrangements (Harvey, 1989). This process is known as time–space compression;
- advancements in technologies of information and communication;
- changes in transport and speed of transit;
- increased migration;
- rise (and fall) of the world economy, market forces and expansion of capitalism; and
- shared issues confronting the world's populations, such as global warming, fractured communities and child poverty.

In simple terms, globalization means that the world has been compressed in terms of time and space, so economic, cultural and political changes have become globally interconnected. Advances in communication and transportation technologies have been at the forefront of this transformation (Brown and Lauder, 1996).

Socio-economic dimension of globalization

There are different dimensions to globalization such as its cultural and political forms, but the focus here will be on the socio-economic dimension. This is important because of the way that economic imperatives are being inserted into the education system and the way in which education is seen to play a crucial role helping each nation's future economic prosperity. Moreover, increased opportunities for interaction mean that education around the world is changing (Brown and Lauder, 1996; Stromquist and Monkman, 2000).

Before the 1970s manufacturing and production used to be carried out domestically; non-industrialized nations were predominantly the sources of raw materials. The international import and export of goods has expanded world markets and established a global economy (Gottdiener and Hutchison, 2006). Economic success and failure are no longer defined by national borders as the global system of capital casts its influence. Many business corporations in industrialized nations have relocated manufacturing around the world in order to find the cheapest way to manufacture their goods. Reich points out: 'Modern factories and state-of-the-art machinery can be installed almost anywhere on the globe' (1997: 163) and standardized products can now be produced around the world. The emphasis is on quality, productivity, outsourcing, investment and capital accumulation.

It is the major global cities, such as Tokyo, London and New York (Sassen, 1991), rather than the nations themselves or other older imperial cities, that are the key centres in the world economy. Hamnett (2003: 24) refers to the global cities as 'The control and command centres of global capitalism'. Furthermore, Baronov (2006) claims that in the US (and other advanced economies) the gap between the wealthy and poor has increased as a result of the development of the global city. Baronov (2006) points out that the wealthy have more in common with the wealthy in other nations than the poor in their own nation. Global economy and trade that links them and their shared characteristics of wealth bring them closer. These global cities operate in the main from the city centre core because that is where key activities take place. Gottdiener and Hutchison (2006) claim that at other times cities change their nature and function to become 'multicentred regions' and the global city forms a part of this expanded global cosmopolitan environment.

While not all nations are experiencing the levels of growth found in the most industrialized nations, all nations are subject to significant changes in the process of urban development, where disinvestment in one urban area is linked with increased investment in another (Giddens, 1990). Urban expansion occurs unevenly with growth slower in the older, industrialized nations than in economically emerging nations such as India and Brazil (United Nations, 2007). These nations are experiencing rapid increases in urban population following the pattern in Europe and the US that began in the eighteenth century. The impact of globalization means that people migrate to cities for jobs. Following investment and economic activities some urban regions, for example in East Asia, have surfaced as highly technical areas of post-industrial growth. Such developments have, however, impacted negatively on rural areas in terms of diminishing workforce and declining community cohesion (Glaeser, 1998; Lipman, 2004).

Global trends of neo-liberal economic policies and the pursuit of individualistic perspectives in the last 30 years or so have resulted in a reduction in care and concern for 'the public good' in public welfare services, such as education and health (Ball et al., 2000). The prevailing discourse has focused on choice, individual competition and profit. In the US context, Castells (1998: 161) claims that this discursive shift is represented by 'a sharp divide between valuable and non-valuable people and locales'. Some older urban locales have become rusty reminders of past industrial success, organized labour and community and now are named as areas of poverty, lacking economic opportunities, peopled with fragmented communities with little hope of recovery.

Activity

To which urban populations is the socio-economic dimension of globalization arguably more advantageous and to which is it less advantageous? You may like to consider issues of social class, shifting demographics and gender.

To what extent are your answers confined to your own geographical context and to what extent can they be transferable to other contexts?

Diverse, changing and fluid communities

In contemporary urban settings the globalizing process creates irregularities; significant demographic changes affect some neighbourhoods and communities, in some cases reviving local cultural identities and in others fracturing traditional social and cultural norms and practices (Giddens, 1999). For example, the impact of immigration on formerly homogenous societies has resulted in a shift in demographics. As migrants tend to settle in urban areas, it is these areas that are most affected.

In some respects, rather than unifying the world, globalization may have polarized it. Wilson (1996) believes that this is particularly the case in the poorest urban communities where people have become isolated due to the globalization of jobs and services have become fragmented. The urban landscape is often one where poverty and affluence exist side by side. It is claimed that the process of globalization has resulted in greater economic and social inequalities and spatial segregation among urban populations (Bodnar, 2007). There are enormous contradictions and inequalities in all cities, where there is great wealth and poverty, inclusion and exclusion (Rizvi and Lingard, 2000; Lipman, 2004). This is evidenced, for example, by the uneven economic opportunities between highly paid middle-class professionals and low-paid-working-class service workers (Anyon, 1997). Reich states that an individual's 'Real competitive position in the world economy is coming to depend on the function you perform in it' (1997: 163) – what Giddens describes as 'A world of winners and losers, a few on the fast track to prosperity, the majority condemned to a life of misery and despair' (1999: 15).

Furthermore, the collapse of the economic and political significance of some inner cities has resulted in isolation of those working-class residents who have remained. The flight of some regularly employed middle and working class families from the inner city, particularly in the US, has meant reduced employment opportunities and greater atomization of those who remain (Jameson, 1991; Wilson, 1991). The most socially and economically excluded have become more permanent in certain parts of the inner city (Mingione, 1996). Moreover, segregation of urban populations is reinforced with the movement of some of the more wealthy inhabitants to the suburbs and partial gentrification of the inner city centre results in a lack of affordable housing.

The economic and social divide and uneven development within cities signifies what has been termed the *dual city* (Castells, 1998).

A concentration of poverty and crime in large cities has reduced the quality of life for some of the population and has made some areas become uninhabitable. According to Gottdiener and Hutchison (2006), the greatest collapse, social isolation and decline in living conditions is to be found in inner cities in the US. In the US, poverty is primarily concentrated in the industrial Northeast and Midwest, where unemployment and social dislocation have increased. Turning to the UK, it has been claimed that there is more poverty here than in most other northern European nations and this is related to worklessness and low pay maintained by the continual importing of cheap labour (OECD, 2001). Using the measure of net household income after housing costs, 20 per cent of people in the UK are poor (Nickell, 2004).

Urban poverty has increased because of changes in production, the relocation of manufacturing industries, various recessions and globalization. The loss of job security is particularly felt among unskilled, unqualified workers in industrialized nations who would previously have been employed in the manufacturing industries prior to the shift in production to economically emerging nations (Reich, 1997). In the case of the US, Wilson (1997: 750) states that poverty and deprivation have 'Become more urban, more concentrated, and more firmly implanted in large metropolises, particularly in the older industrial cities'. Policy supports this inequality by legitimizing the movement of cheap labour, while the social cost of the worklessness that is thus caused is borne not by the corporations but by communities, who have the least economic and social capital to respond (Bourdieu and Passeron, 1979).

Indeed, in modern urban communities, including both industrialized and emerging cities, there are many dull and repetitive jobs that require unskilled and inexpensive labour. This work is often done by those in the lowest and most socially and economically disadvantaged and disenfranchised stratum of society (Gilbert, 1998). Furthermore, migrant communities from non-industrialized nations, moving to nations or communities in the hope of there being better opportunities and benefits, are often required to take the lowest paying jobs, often in service jobs and downgraded, manufacturing industries (Sassen, 2006). Grace (1994) argues that this division of labour makes the lives of *the contented electoral majority* more comfortable with little interest in improving the social welfare, well-being or social rights of the poor. This is further exacerbated by a deliberate process of demonizing and further marginalizing the working classes of all ethnicities.

Activity

What can be done individually and/or collectively to take advantage of and embrace, or mitigate against, the consequences of globalization?

How can marginalized and excluded people in urban contexts mobilize to improve their situation?

The impact of the forces of globalization on urban education

It has been claimed that it is difficult to assess the effects of globalization on education because of the lack of agreement about what the term actually means, as discussed earlier in this chapter (Lauder et al., 2006). However, what does seem to emerge is an inherent contradiction. Dominant lines of reasoning are based around notions of a globally competitive market place chasing a cheap labour force. Yet, education is also seen to play a crucial role with the concern to produce a highly educated workforce (Brown and Lauder, 1996). Indeed, in the UK context, the government has stated that: 'To compete in the global economy . . . we will have to unlock the potential of every young person' (DfEE, 1997b: 3). According to this dominant view, 'the only type of worker who matters is the highly educated one' (Sassen, 2006: 11). Hence there is a clear relationship between education, jobs and the rewards for those who are perceived to have value in the production of economic prosperity in the global labour market. Moreover, 'According to the market rules of engagement, the prosperity of workers will depend on an ability to trade their skills, knowledge and entrepreneurial acumen in an unfettered global market-place' (Brown and Lauder, 1996: 49). The manifestation of this is felt most heavily by those who are unable or unwilling to embrace these so-called opportunities.

One effect of globalisation on education is that, as societies continue to change and evolve as part of broader economic developments, more emphasis is placed on the insertion of neo-liberal quasi-market principles such as regulation, the raising of standards and accountability. Hence many nations have moved to reform their public educational provision, in order to raise measurable attainment levels, create different types of schools and encourage competition and choice in order allegedly to increase international competitiveness (Ball, 2008).

This concentration on the global economization of education fails to take into account alternative local, regional and cultural discourses. A focus on education provision preoccupied with raising standards means that there are questions about the extent to which all groups have either the desire or are equipped to acquire the educational means to achieve potential. It can be argued that education is a lot more than this. Indeed, Baronov states that concentrating on uniformity of the curriculum, standardized testing and school ranking, downplay the role of the learning process, producing a generation 'prepared to join a homogeneous and interchangeable global workforce' (2006: 16).

It is partly the responsibility of any education system to prepare a skilled workforce that can enter the employment market. However, de-industrialization and the emergence of a technological rather than an industrial/manufacturing society, at least in the West meant a change in emphasis towards a workforce responding to the demands of a post-industrial world. As Ball (2006: 68) claims: 'Not everyone has an equal "stake" in the success of the new economic order.' The result is a more segmented and polarized workforce based on those workers central to globalization and those on the periphery, a parallel that Ball sees in 'School polarisations within "market reformed" education systems'.

Although these issues do not just relate to the urban context, Gulson claims the interaction between education and the everyday practices of populations 'shape, and are shaped by, physical locations, particularly cities' (2005: 142). Indeed, Sassen (2006: 12) claims that cities have surfaced 'as a lens for research and theorisation about a broad array of major social, cultural, economic, and political processes central to the current era'. Writing about the US, Lipman (2004) maintains that economic restructuring policies operate to reinforce inequalities, widening the gap between those (urban) schools serving low-income, working-class students and those serving more affluent populations. Similarly, this differentiation produces a workforce that is economically and culturally stratified and fragmented.

Furthermore, it is claimed that a neo-liberal politics favours the middle class in terms of selection and the attainment of credentials as not all social groups have the same advantages (Reay, 2006). The consequence of such an approach results in the segregation of children into different types of schools based on social class. The middle classes are better positioned than the working classes to provide a 'good' education for their children (Ball, 2008). Referring to the US context, Lipman claims: 'This stratified education produces identities for a stratified labor force, stratified city, and stratified society' (2004: 174). Indeed, changes to employment opportunities for young people have increased problems for schools, particularly in working-class neighbourhoods (Ball et al., 2000). On leaving school, many of those working-class young people, who lack formal qualifications, may fill low-skilled, poorly paid jobs. In a globalizing economy, much low-skilled work has moved from de-industrializing societies to the newly industrialized centres, resulting in the northern hemisphere societies fighting over high-skilled jobs and increased competition for the remaining low-skilled jobs. Furthermore, the expansion of higher education in low-wage paying economies has resulted in a high-skilled, low-paid or unemployed workforce (Brown and Lauder, 1997). The knowledge-based economy, as a result of globalization, has increased competition for higher paid jobs among graduates and the need to train and retrain in order to keep up with technological innovations. This further opens up education to be co-modified and reduced to 'discrete, reified, and ultimately saleable things or packages of things' (Noble, 2002: 3).

One further point is worth considering here in relation to the construction and role of the teacher in the globalization process. As the relationship between globalization and education evolves, to what extent is the role of the teacher changing in order to fulfil the needs of the globalizing economy? Internationally, contemporary teacher reforms are driven by governmental agenda about skills, competencies and accountability that make an 'effective' homogeneous teacher, responsible for producing the requirements of the labour market. In this (re)construction of the teacher, alternative identities and values have been sidelined; for instance, a commitment to 'the common good' and preparation for 'being a teacher' in a challenging urban school setting. The neo-liberal, globalizing agenda that is impacting on education policy is increasingly taking away the autonomy and creativity of the teacher in many urban settings. Nevertheless, it should be recognized that 'the construction of the teacher is always context dependent – the teacher is always produced out of local histories, cultures and politics' (Maguire, 2010, in press).

Activity

Brainstorm the needs of an urban dweller in a globalized society.
How is education meeting those needs? How is it currently failing to meet those needs?

Glocal urban education programmes

In terms of studying contemporary cities in any part of the world, what happens locally is also influenced by factors across the globe and what people do locally is also part of the process of reproducing globalization. 'There can be no such thing as globalisation without the global penetration of the local. The penetration of the local is what makes globalisation global' (Spybey, 2001: 157). So globalization is a dual, interactive process – 'thinking globally and acting locally' that has been referred to as 'glocalization' (Robertson, 1995). The impact of the economic form of globalization produces an escalation of new relations between locales, which 'link distant localities in such a way that local happenings are shaped by events occurring many miles away and vice versa' (Giddens, 1990: 64). From an urban education perspective, it is necessary to treat local knowledge seriously but also to draw on research into world cities (Sassen, 1991).

This section provides some examples of education programmes that urban communities around the world are undertaking to bring about change in the light of globalization. As Anyon explains of the US (1997: 170): 'The aim is to create conditions for ghetto residents that will allow them to feel the sense of personal agency and self-determination that results from real economic and political possibilities – more common for middle-class and affluent families.' Social movements, such as the Association of Community Organisations for Reform Now (ACORN) in the US and The Brazilian Landless People's Movement (MST) have evolved 'providing glimpses of possible futures and are in some part vehicles for their realisation' (Giddens, 1990: 161). These social movements aim to counter the hegemony of the dominant neo-liberal education policies. They can offer socially transformative alternatives to the dominance of current forms of globalization by raising critical awareness and using democratic participation for future, sustainable development: 'not a precipitous transformation but a slow, long-term process of incremental, cumulative changes that will increase the capabilities of citizens to address the problems they face' (Van Vliet, 2002: 40).

Many of the well-known community-based education programmes have been based around progressive political thinking from Europe and Latin America. They are aimed at improving the lives of ordinary people through democratic change and developments and by making the link between education and direct social action through consciousness-raising and mobilization of urban communities. A key exponent of this approach was Paulo Freire (1970 – discussed in Chapter 7).

These local responses to counteract globalizing neo-liberal influences are happening in many nations. Such initiatives explore: 'a very different vision of the place of the school in society and of curricula, teaching, and evaluation' (Gandin, 2004: 1) to transform classrooms and schools to better serve the community. A study by Kruger and Chawla (2002) of four areas in Johannesburg used UNESCO's 'growing up in cities' model to solicit the views of 10- to 14-year-old children about how Johannesburg could be improved, by evaluating the urban environment and the conditions of their lives, measured against international indicators. Children's perspectives and experience from four different areas in Johannesburg were studied and it was found that there was no single urban experience but there was some cause for alarm as neighbourhoods were hostile and the city areas were not child friendly, which meant the children lived constrained lives and there were considerable risks. Some small changes would result in the transformation of their living conditions, such as providing safe play spaces and clearing up rubbish. The study recommended that adults could make the difference to the children's lives – and unified commitment was required from government, communities and families to improve the situation and build social change. Such knowledge and understanding impacts both globally and nationally, in terms of drawing parallels with elsewhere, as well as providing the initiative to pressurize for local sustained development.

Riley points out that schools particularly in urban contexts, can better meet their educational aims when they have the support of the local community and a reciprocal trusting relationship is built up (Riley, 2008). The Rethinking Schools Project in Milwaukee is based around the teacher journal 'Rethinking Schools'. It provides readers with the opportunity to learn about social justice and anti-racist issues. The contributions to the journal are from teachers and the examples they offer are based on alternative education practices that counter dominant neo-liberal policies. From a broader perspective on human development and enhancement, their objective is to look beyond education as merely seeing it for the purpose of generating economic growth and prosperity (Sen, 1997), but as a life-long capability.

Movement building can also begin in the urban schools themselves in order to provide a high-quality education. In Philadelphia, Anyon (1997; 2005) describes small, self-contained learning communities within large comprehensive high schools based on teachers organizing students into a city-wide Student Union (PSU). Decentralization of administration has resulted in school-based student governments responsible for decision-making, local management of resources and campaigning to increase school funding.

Van Vliet (2002) describes how cities can act not just in terms of growth but also agents for greater social justice and environmental sustainability. He talks of *liveable cities*, with their roots in participatory democracy and partnerships. He maintains that: 'The promise for improving urban liveability rests on freeing the potential of people living in poverty' (2002: 31). Liveable cities are:

> Places where residents can find jobs that pay a living wage. A liveable city provides its citizens with basic services, including safe water and adequate sanitation. The inhabitants of a liveable city have access to educational opportunities and health care. (p. 34)

However, dominant globalizing practices based on economic competition can constrain liveability. Therefore social justice and environmental sustainability need to be pursued and new approaches need to be found that deliver what is needed for the common good. But this 'depends in equal measure on the extent to which communities and civil society groups can build ties with people and agencies within the state who share the same agenda' (p. 40). This necessitates a long-term process of change that will support the people as equal partners in addressing the problems themselves and by building partnerships and advocacy with both public and private enterprise to support projects.

One of the most notable examples of an urban community working together for change has been in Brazil. Since 1989, the Escola Cidada (The Citizen School Project) in Porto Alegre has provided education for poor children and citizens in a city in southern Brazil, the state capital of Rio Grande do Sul. This alternative education is based on inclusive democratic policies and shared values, challenging those neo-liberal global policies found at national level. Furthermore, the project has a global political aim of the emancipation and social transformation of poor people worldwide drawing on the alternative values and ideas of Freire, based on empowerment, solidarity and democratizing schooling and education policies. The project (now adopted as a system in the municipal borough of Rio Grande do Sul) aimed to create better education opportunities for the poorest children excluded by the state from education in impoverished, urban neighbourhoods in this part of Brazil, to encourage innovation and prioritize valuable, justifiable knowledge in the school setting. Included among the initiatives is the redistribution of funding to the poorest and most needy areas such as in the favelas or shanty towns. The local communities are involved in the administration, budgeting and management by setting up organizations to enable full involvement at grassroots level.

In educational terms, this initiative has involved all the stakeholders in the municipal schools such as students, parents and community as well as administrators and educators being involved in goal-setting, decision-making and design about what they want school to be like and how they want it to be run. This project is in contrast to increased national centralization, the privatization of social programmes, increased state regulation of citizens and reduced autonomy, which have affected those people from working-class, low-income backgrounds in other parts of Brazil. These emancipatory policies and practices are political choices which can have an impact on the lives of the learners. The international interest in the Porto Alegre education model demonstrates the impact the local can have on the global (Gandin and Apple, 2003).

'The Escola Cidada operated from the fundamental premise that democratizing schools requires a collective effort to create an educational project that is open and flexible in its structures while maintaining its goals of radically democratizing school practices' (Gandin and Fischman, 2006: 138). This includes involving the excluded and impoverished population in making decisions about what actually counts as knowledge, articulated through forms of pedagogy and in the curriculum based on the real experiences of the school community. The process has also been responsible for the creation of new organizations in other aspects of social life in the neighbourhoods, creating new relations between the state, schools and communities and 'educating' and empowering impoverished people – for instance, in real terms, giving them greater opportunities in the labour market is one way to help provide solutions to their problems (Gandin, 2004; Apple and Beane, 2007).

Activity

What are the opportunities or limitations of extending the above educational initiatives within your national or local context?
How might these be influenced by social class, ethnicity and gender?

Conclusion

There is a lack of understanding or agreement about the nature of globalization and its consequences. According to some explanations, the world market is replacing the control of the nation-state; other explanations claim the nation-state maintains a degree of control which can bring with it new local pressures (Giddens, 1999).

Education is seen as essential for future economic prosperity in the world market and therefore education policy is strongly influenced by globalization discourses, or at least neo-liberal economics. The primary focus, certainly in the West, has been on producing a labour force that complements the needs of the post-industrial world. However, as Ball claims, 'the idea of globalisation has to be treated with care' (2008: 25) in terms of the key issues it raises for education, for instance the changes in the labour market and how this may affect schools in working-class districts (Willis, 2006). Is it reasonable for education to carry this responsibility?

Economic globalization has not been experienced equally. To take the case of the urban education context, since 2008, for the first time, half of the world population now lives in urban areas and this is increasing. By 2050, it is predicted 70 per cent of the population will be urban (United Nations, 2007). Urban areas are connected by a global economy but development is uneven and unequal. Consequently, there are contradictions in the way in which globalization is experienced. While there is greater interconnectedness between urban areas in terms of global capital, there is also disconnectedness to the social issues and needs of local urban communities.

The chapter has made suggestions for developing both existing and new social movements in urban areas that can work towards greater social justice. Examples such as The Escola Cidada in Porto Alegre show that the neo-liberal globalizing agenda is not inevitable. Urban education and urban educators are at the centre of such efforts. Governmental initiatives have attempted, through a neo-liberal ideology, to improve schools. However, this chapter has indicated the limitations of these processes. Life in the cities will only be improved by public action and social movements to force an appropriate political response. As Lipman (2004: 4) claims: 'What is at stake are not only the educational experiences and life chances of students, but the kind of city and the kind of society we will have' or indeed we now have.

Further reading

Apple, M. W. (ed.) (2003) *The State and the Politics of Knowledge.* London: RoutledgeFalmer. Chapter 8 written with Luis Armando Gandin discusses The Citizen School Project in Porto Alegre, Brazil.

Brighouse, T. and Fullick, L. (eds) (2007) *Education in a Global City.* London: Institute of Education.

Globalisation, Societies and Education, a journal published by Routledge, Taylor and Francis Group

Lauder, H., Brown, P., Dillabough, J. and Halsey, A. (eds) (2006) *Education, Globalization and Social Change*. Oxford: Oxford University Press.

Useful websites

http://globalresearch.ca/
Centre for Research on Globalization
http://uk.oneworld.net/
One World Globalisation Guide
http://www.unesco.org.uk/
United Nations Educational, Scientific and Cultural Organization

6 Policies in Urban Settings

Introduction

Policy is sometimes thought of as being the formal and legislative 'plans for education developed by politicians and their advisors' (Maguire and Dillon, 2007: 29). These are plans that will generally have 'consequences for institutions and practitioners who are required to accept policy as a guide for action' (Ozga, 2000: 56). However, understanding policy in a more critical sense involves seeing policy as a 'politically, socially and historically contextualised practice or set of practices' (Olssen et al., 2004: 3). It involves questions about why a particular approach has been taken; who has reached this decision; how the policy been challenged or interpreted; what have been the outcomes, both expected and unexpected, of a particular policy intervention? There is always a historical dimension to policy-making (Gale, 2001). Not surprisingly, there are many overlaps between current UK policy-making and older policy discourses surrounding the 'unruly' inner city (Ball, 2008). There is also a socio-political aspect to policy-making in terms of power and control to define the terms and reach of the policy 'problems' and any 'solutions'. Thus, in this chapter, while we want to describe some of the urban policies that are currently in circulation, we also want to raise questions about why some policies, and not others, are more likely to be advocated.

The origins of urban education policy

There have always been concerns about the urban poor. Writing of the nineteenth-century urban policy and its overlaps with current forms, Ball (2008: 56) argues that 'The "urban" was then and is now a repository and magnifier of social problems'. Sometimes the urban working classes have been 'blamed' for their poverty and deprivation; sometimes they have been 'pitied' for these same conditions (Jones and Novak, 1999). Education and training, particularly of a vocational nature, have always been seen and continue to be seen as a partial policy solution to poverty. Helping people to help themselves through work has an enduring history in the UK (Stedman-Jones, 2004). But the form that educational policy intervention has taken has often been shaped by ideologies of differentiation, separation and segregation.

Although we do not have enough space to do justice to the origins of state schooling – the schools that were set up by the 1870 Elementary School Act – these schools were only for the children of the working classes (Silver, 1983). The campaign to set these schools up and support them through taxation was contested as there were middle-class concerns about 'over-educating' those who were expected to maintain a lowly place in society. Working-class children were exposed to a sometimes brutish and impoverished school system. There were some teachers, philanthropists and organized workers who challenged this harsh, stultifying regime. Political struggles centred on the need to reduce child labour and to provide free meals for the 'large numbers of children . . . attending school in a state of near starvation' (Simon, 1974: 133). The purpose of these schools was clear: 'the elementary schools of 1870 were intended in the main to produce an orderly, civil, obedient population, with sufficient education to understand a command' (Tawney, 1924: 22, cited in Simon, 1974: 119).

What we see at the inception of state schooling is a policy of segregated provision aimed at the urban working classes who were seen as a 'problem', a threat to the middle classes and to social order. This segregated provision was 'disrupted' to a minor degree by a form of selection that was introduced by scholarship examinations. Elementary school children who passed the scholarship examinations could go to the local fee-paying Secondary Schools, attended, in the main, by middle-class children. Although working-class children would have their fees paid by the scholarship fund, they had to fund equipment, books and uniforms. Many working-class children who passed the examinations were unable to take up their scholarships and instead went out to work. In some parts of the country, there were Higher Elementary Schools that were successfully making the case for universal Secondary education for all, but these were thinly spread in the cities of the late nineteenth and early twentieth century (Simon, 1974). In terms of politics, culture and ideologies, segregated and differentiated provision for the children of the poor and working classes was the order of the day – albeit with a small provision for 'rescuing' those talented enough to pass the scholarship exam (the notion of 'rescuing' those deemed able to benefit from a more academic curriculum still enjoys a degree of policy continuity to this day).

Activity

To what extent do any contemporary education policies that you can identify, contain echoes of older discourses of classed segregation?

This brief overview of the educational policy response to the nineteenth-century 'threat' of the urban working classes (Hall, 1977) highlights an attempt to 'gentle' and control a potentially unruly class. The English middle classes were anxious about the urban unrest, political agitations and trade union activism that threatened their way of life (Stedman-Jones, 1992). The provision of schooling of any sort worked as a lever for raising expectations for more and better education and for further social reform. During the passage of the twentieth century, the aspirations and struggles of the organized working classes, the activities of the teachers' trade unions and the campaigning of socialist politicians and many urban philanthropists kept the concerns for the urban poor on the political and moral agenda (McCulloch, 2007). However, it was not until the landslide success of the Labour Movement and the formation of Clement Atlee's post-war government in 1945 when major social policy reforms were enacted (Timmins, 1996).

In the early part of the twentieth century, Atlee had worked in the boys' clubs of the East End of London. There he saw the privations of poverty and deprivation. He never forgot this urban experience and he was determined to challenge this state of affairs through political action. His early campaigning concentrated on reducing poverty through increasing employment opportunities. Under his premiership, the Education Act of 1944 provided free Secondary schooling for all children for the first time in the UK. Due to political struggles between different policy stakeholders (over the role of the Church in education provision as well as concerns about what sort of schooling was appropriate for the masses) the Act resulted in a settlement of segregated and differentiated provision (McCulloch, 1994). The grammar schools (academic in nature and largely serving a middle-class intake) were brought into the state system. Secondary Modern schools were set up and generally catered for working-class children. There were also supposed to be some technical schools, designed to provide skills training and vocational preparation, although few of these were set up.

Much of the research that has explored who went to the three different types of schools has demonstrated, in no uncertain terms, that working-class children were disproportionately placed in less academic schools (Halsey et al., 1980). Lacey's (1970) study of High Town Grammar School found that even when working-class boys did access the more academic grammar schools, they were likely to underachieve in relation to their measured capabilities when contrasted with middle-class boys who had come to the grammar schools with lower measured aptitudes. So, while policies such as the 1944 Education Act were enacted to ameliorate some educational inequalities, at least in terms of access to Secondary Schooling, what was provided was still segregated through discourses of meritocracy ('ability') that worked to ensure the continuation, in the main, of a class differentiated provision. Although the great cities contained many high-status selective grammar schools, the urban working-class child was more likely to attend the less well-funded and vocationally oriented Secondary Modern School.

The post-war years were a time of full employment due to the reconstruction work that was taking place to rebuild bombed areas and produce a 'land fit for heroes'. However, wages were low and social benefits were limited. Poor housing, poor health and poverty had not been removed by the welfare state, although their worse effects had been reduced (Timmins, 1996). But the inner cities were changing in other ways. The post-war 'baby boom' was putting pressure on welfare provision such as schools and healthcare. In this period, the movement of ex-Commonwealth people back to their 'motherland', after successfully gaining national independence in many cases, was also to influence urban policy and practice. These men and women, who were recruited to fill vacancies in the UK labour market, were not initially eligible for state housing. As has always been the pattern for sojourners and settlers, these communities settled in urban areas where they were able to find work, affordable accommodation and schools for their children close to their friends and members of their families (Fryer, 1984).

During the late 1950s and early 1960s, educational commentators and researchers started to document the achievement of children in state schools. It became apparent that there were patterns of classed attainment that were regulated by an 'emphasis on processes of sorting and grading' (Williams, 1961: 170). There was a concern that 'poor boys [sic] of exceptional ability might not get their "chance", might be wasted' (Williams, 1961: 170). In all this, the only measure of 'success' was academic achievement; vocational achievement has never been celebrated in the same way. There was also a fear that urban working-class youth was unruly and a challenge to social cohesion. In particular, the rise of working-class youth subcultures such as Teddy Boys and, later on, Mods and Rockers, was seen as a threat to law and order and stability (Skelton and Valentine, 1998). However, in the 1960s an influential change in social consciousness crossed the Atlantic which had critical implications for urban education.

Urban policy and the welfare state

During the early 1960s in the US, there was an upsurge in social movements for change that were eventually reflected in the UK. The civil rights movement in the US was the spur for a heightened awareness of continued exclusions and oppressions. It was also the catalyst for urban uprisings and agitations. Together with the international campaign that opposed the US military intervention in Vietnam, it seemed that power did indeed belong to the people (a popular slogan of the day). Changes could be made to social injustices. More egalitarian concerns about poverty, social justice and civil rights started to inflect urban education policy-making. According to Cicirelli, the urban policy approaches of the period fell into three distinct but frequently overlapping clusters (Cicirelli, 1972).

First, Cicirelli argued that much urban policy-making was based on notions of 'deficit' where the underlying premise was that urban children and their families 'lacked' some key essential ingredient that prevented their success in education. For example, not getting the 'right' sort of support from within the family at an early stage in development could, it was argued, compound later underachievement in education. A 'stronger' interpretation of this approach might argue that material disadvantages could and can only be tackled by political responses such as taxation reforms or additional state welfare. A 'weaker' version that 'blamed' the culture of the family would be more likely to result in policies based on supplementing the so-called deficits (Mills and Gale, 2004). One indirect consequence of the 'weaker' policy approach that dominated the UK in the 1960s, and has continued to influence urban policy, was that it inadvertently signalled that urban working-class families and communities needed the help of professionals in order to manage their lives (Corson, 1998).

Cicirelli catalogued a second policy approach that focused on differences between similar urban schools. It was argued that some schools, which allegedly shared similar intakes to less successful schools, were achieving better results. This approach indirectly 'blamed' the less successful school. It also meant that any politics of redistribution (increased welfare benefits; better funding to 'disadvantaged' schools) were less likely to be advocated. If some schools were doing well without any additional financial support, then all schools should be able to cope. This approach has continued to characterize some of the mainstream schools improvement discourse in the UK (Thrupp, 2005; Raffo, 2009). If some schools in challenging circumstances can 'succeed' then other similar schools should be able to do the same.

Cicirelli identified a third policy approach of helping students to overcome disadvantage through generating positive views about themselves and their capacity to succeed. It could be argued that in this approach, the 'blame' for underachievement still rested with the individual child and their family and their alleged low self-esteem. It could also be argued that this perspective displaced the impact of poverty, poor health and poor housing on attainment (Grace, 1995). In the UK, Stone (1985) successfully demonstrated that black children were not lower in self-esteem than their white peers, a claim that was frequently used to 'explain' different levels of attainment and that sidelined the ways in which racism, exclusion and low expectations in schools had contributed to their reduced attainment (Stone 1985; see also Gillborn, 1997 and Archer and Francis, 2007).

Activity

What current education policies can you identify that fall into Cicerelli's framework of 'deficit'; 'school-centred' and 'individually-located'?

These three policy approaches underpinned various education policy attempts to reduce the 'achievement gap' between urban working-class children and middle-class children in the US and the UK in the 1960s. Policies took two main forms, compensation and intervention; many policies incorporated both of these strands. In the US, one of the best-known compensatory-interventionist strategies was the Head Start programme based on interventions for young children, such as breakfast clubs, in an attempt to compensate for their disadvantaged start to life. Another (slightly later) intervention was the Reading Recovery programme set up by Marie Clay in New Zealand that quickly spread to many urban areas to assist 'disadvantaged' children overcome early literacy difficulties (Clay, 1982). In the UK, in the mid 1960s, the Educational Priority Area (EPA) schemes put some additional funds into schools that served 'deprived' areas. The sums involved were very small and the scheme was not supported for very long (Tomlinson, 2005).

By the 1970s and into the 1980s in the UK, any radical concerns about the need to combat poverty and inequality in education (and society) were gradually replaced (in policy terms at least) by a market discourse that privileged choice, competition and standards (Maguire and Dillon, 2007). In this new policy setting, the educational focus shifted to individual competition and testing rather than combating the effects of poverty and deprivation. However, social inequalities did not go away (Walker and Walker, 1997). In the UK when New Labour came to power in 1997 it set up the Social Exclusion Unit: urban education was back on the policy agenda.

New Labour, challenging schools and urban policy: phase 1

New Labour set up the Social Exclusion Unit in order to 'repair the social damage of the previous two decades' (Jones, 2003: 145). Raffo (2009: 65) puts it like this:

> Following a period in the 1990s in which issues around disadvantage and the relationship between poverty and low educational achievement were, arguably, under-played in England, New Labour policy since 1997 has once again begun to take these issues seriously.

Measures such as the minimum wage, working family tax credits and increased pensioner credits were put into place in order to tackle exclusion and poverty. New Labour set in place a campaign to abolish child poverty by 2020. Toynbee was able to claim that whereas in 2006 the UK was the worst in the European Union for childhood poverty, by 2006, the UK was 'at the EU average and improving fastest' (2006).

New Labour developed a range of education welfare policies like Sure Start and Family Literacy to support parents before their children started school. There were some tax breaks and increases in benefit payments to some of the poorer families in the UK. New Labour argued that some schools were more successful than others and needed to be emulated, through, for example, the Beacon Schools Programme. They also identified Primary Schools that showed what they called 'leading practice' (DfEE, 1997b). New Labour also took up some of the ideas of raising self-esteem and aspirations particularly through mentoring approaches which it adopted 'as an intervention with disadvantaged young people' (Colley, 2003: 1). However, in spite of these interventions, research has shown that the children of the poor still achieve less than their middle-class peers (Ennals, 2004; Hirsch, 2007). 'Our cities fail to provide the quality of life which our wealth as a society should be able to create for all' (Johnson, 1999: 49). In terms of an urban policy analysis, there has been a degree of continuity over time in respect of urban education policy as many of these interventions mirror Cicirelli's three policy approaches.

The Sure Start programme (DfEE, 1999b) offers support for families in 'disadvantaged areas' from pregnancy through to when the child is 14. Sure Start's concerns, as detailed on their website, are with 'improving health and emotional development for young children' and 'supporting parents as parents and in their aspirations towards employment' (www.surestart.gov.uk). Children's Centres and Early Excellence Centres, one-stop shops to offer advice and support in the areas of education, health and welfare have also been set up. The Children Act (2004) and Children Trusts are intended to work alongside the Every Child Matters (Great Britain, 2003) policy. While these sorts of policies reflect the US Head Start interventions and are (perhaps) based on a 'deficit' view, the policy intention is to support and sustain improvement through working *with* families rather than *on* them through 'correcting' or 'blaming'. However, work and employment are still seen as corrective devices in the eradication of poverty. The goals of many of these policies are couched in economic rather than socially just outcomes.

Two specific urban projects were enacted when New Labour came into government: the Education Action Zone (EAZ) projects and the Excellence in Cities (EiC) initiative. EAZs were set up (DfEE, 1997b; DfEE, 1999a) to raise standards in areas of high disadvantage. The intention was to attract funding and expertise from the private business sector in order to inject a sense of entrepreneurialism and foster success in schools facing challenging circumstances. EAZs supported a range of different activities in schools such as breakfast clubs and classes where newly arrived parents could learn English. Many of the strategies set up under the EAZ umbrella were similar to those of the Education Priority Areas in the 1960s. However, there were no significant gains in test scores in the EAZ schools (Reid and Brain, 2003; West et al., 2003) – although 'gains' take time to achieve and need to be nurtured and supported by long-term funding, as with the Head Start work in the US. The EAZs were quietly allowed to 'wither on the vine' and were incorporated into the EiC project.

EiC (DfEE, 1999) initially specified six conurbations – London, Birmingham, Manchester, Liverpool, Leeds and Sheffield, where a wide range of policies were to be directed. These included a commitment to provide a learning mentor for 'every young person who needs one, as a single point of contact to tackle barriers to students' learning' (DfEE, 1999: 3). Whitty (2002) has claimed that one of the potential strengths in EiC was that it targeted *all* children. It was hoped that in-school strategies such as streaming as well as extending opportunities for 'gifted and talented' children could attract and retain the supposedly supportive and pro-school middle-class children in city schools. As with the EAZs, by 2003, the chief inspector of schools reported that although EiC had enhanced student confidence, educational gains in terms of test scores were less evident (Bell, 2003). While the EAZs and EiC made contributions in schools through funding breakfast clubs, parent groups and learning mentors, it might have been unrealistic to expect low-cost interventions to achieve much more than this in the short term (Ainscow and West, 2006).

In 2004, New Labour published its 'Five year strategy for Children and learners' (DfES, 2004). This 'radical' document set out a wide number of proposals to tackle disadvantage and underachievement from under-five provision through to the 'world of work'. The centrepiece of this policy document was the promise of a set of privately sponsored schools (Academy Schools) that would be 'located in areas of disadvantage' in order to 'break the cycle of underachievement in areas of social and economic deprivation' (DfES, 2006a). Academy Schools are controversial. For example, Mortimore (2007: 4) has asked whether they are the 'most hopeful way of tackling the challenges of inner city schooling' or just 'another expensive, incremental stage in the eventual privatisation of our education system'. Academies weaken the capacity of local education authorities to plan and organize strategically in their areas. In exchange for two million pounds (although this requirement has now been dropped), sponsors are entrusted with many responsibilities, such as setting up the governing body and staff recruitment, without necessarily having an educational background. (One survey has indicated that much of this money was not transferred into the system, Taylor and Evans, 2006.) Above all, there has been some controversy about the claim evidence that the Academy Schools are successful in raising standards for 'disadvantaged' children. The evidence seems to indicate that the Academies that are 'improving' are perhaps 'changing their intake or are not even the most disadvantaged in the area' (Gorard, 2005: 376). As Gorard (2009: 113) has pointed out, Academies will continue to pose a problem for many educationalists: 'their potential for increasing inequity for no gain in attainment will concern us more and more'.

Since coming to power in 1997, New Labour has directed policy attention to 'particular groups, areas and institutions' in areas of disadvantage (Raffo, 2009: 68). It is undoubtedly the case that there have been some improvements and educational gains for some schools (Kendall et al., 2005). However, overwhelmingly, the gains have been small while the evidence has suggested that since 1997, social mobility has not improved (Blanden and Machin, 2007). Intergenerational mobility, the extent to which children can achieve more than their parent's generation, illustrates 'the extent to which a person's circumstances during childhood are reflected in their success in later life, or on the flip-side, the extent to which individuals can make it by virtue of their own talents, motivation and luck' (Blanden et al., 2005). The evidence demonstrates that social mobility decreased for those born in the 1970s as compared with those born in 1958. The evidence currently suggests that while social mobility may not be falling as sharply as it did for the 1970s cohorts, there is little evidence to suggest that there has been much improvement (Chowdry et al., 2009). Social mobility for those in the poorer groups in society remains low.

Buried within this policy discourse of social mobility there is another foundational discourse – that of the notion of individual 'escape' from disadvantage rather than a 'stronger' challenge to economic and social oppressions that sustain inequality, for example, low wages, unemployment and poor housing. Interwoven into these mobility discourses are beliefs and values about what really counts in education: formal accreditation in traditionally academic disciplines.

New Labour, challenging schools and urban policy: phase 2

In his paper entitled 'Twenty years of progress?' Whitty (2008) provides an overview of policies that New Labour has put in place to tackle social exclusion (rather than work to promote social justice). Whitty makes the point that New Labour has been in power for some considerable time, and keynote policies of neo-liberalism and the so-called 'inevitabilistic' force of globalization are still part of New Labour discourse (Cerny and Evans, 2004). However, Whitty argues that there were 'signs that the Brown government that took office in June 2007 may be willing to bring social justice issues further up the agenda' (2008: 180).

In 2007, a number of reports were published that challenged New Labour's claims to have developed a more inclusive society. The Rowntree Report (Dorling et al., 2007) found that under New Labour, inequality had reached levels not seen in the UK for over 40 years. Another study conducted by Taylor and Bradley found that despite many policy attempts to raise standards, such as the EAZs and specialist schools, any gains when set against costs were 'meagre' (cited in Curtis, 2007b). A third set of findings from the review of reforms in Primary schooling, 'The Primary Review', (www.primaryreview. org.uk) suggested that any gains in test scores were largely related to 'teaching to the tests'. The Primary Review also indicated that there had been a limited impact on reading standards despite the National Literacy Strategy. Although there were some 'modest' improvements, what was significant was that in general, progress has been limited in spite of the tremendous volume of central policy interventions aimed at raising standards (Barker, 2008). Whitty believes that the next set of policies will need to take a more socio-political approach:

> New Labour has long seemed to recognize the importance of wider structural and cultural factors in its broader policies, especially in the Sure Start initiative and around the children's agenda, but it has not always applied such insights to its understanding of the differential performance in schools. (Whitty, 2008: 174)

One policy response was the publication of 'The Children's Plan' (DCSF, 2007b: 1) intended to make the UK 'the best place in the world for children and young people to grow up in'. In relation to urban education policy, the Child Poverty Unit was charged with coordinating the attempt to 'halve child poverty by 2010'. One strand tackles the issue of poor housing and over-crowding. Another strand offers 'up to 15 hours of free early education and childcare to 20,000 2 year olds in the most disadvantaged communities' (DCSF, 2007: 9). Young people will be expected to remain in education and training until they are aged 18 or beyond – regardless of their previous experiences that may have included rejection and alienation (Maguire, 2009). Through these sorts of strategies, and others, the intention is to address the complex ways in which 'too many children's education is still being held back by poverty and disadvantage' (DCSF, 2007: 1). While the 'rags and hunger' of earlier times have been abolished (Williams, 1961: 380), inequality is buoyant (Dorling et al., 2007; Wilkinson and Pickett, 2009; Oppenheim, 2009). However Lupton et al. (2009) argue that there have been some small but real gains in alleviating poverty in the New Labour administrations. It remains to be seen if New Labour has reflected on some of the policy failures of its time in power sufficiently well enough to be able to achieve the outcomes suggested in 'The Children's Plan'. What has never been tried is any attempt to challenge and change the education provision, its content and pedagogy, in which so many working-class children seem to 'underachieve'.

In the economic recession of 2008 onwards, and in a context where trust was seriously eroded in the political classes in the UK, New Labour struggled to survive. Part of their strategies of renewal involved the generation of even more education policies. The White Paper, 'Your child, your schools, our future: building a twenty-first century schools system' (DCSF, 2009) signalled the intent to offer more support for children who were 'falling behind'. There was support for more Academy Schools as well as a commitment to break the connections between 'disadvantage and low achievement'. However, radical outcomes will not be achieved by policies that merely deliver 'more of the same'.

Activity

What sorts of policies do you think could make a real difference to urban schools?

Conclusion

In this chapter it has been argued that government policy-making for urban schools in the UK has often, and over an extended period of time, been expressed in individualistic and 'deficit' terms that disregard the impact of the wider social context. There has been a tendency, laid down over time, to 'blame' individual children, their parents, their schools and their teachers for any 'failure' in educational attainment. In asking questions about why certain policies and not others are more likely to be advocated and why the 'problem' is often couched in terms of 'deficits', one explanation may lie in a concern not to challenge or change fundamental social inequalities and injustices. When we examine the policy history of urban schooling, as we have briefly attempted to do in this chapter, and when we critically explore the policies that have been and continue to be designed to deal with the 'problem' of the urban working classes, it is difficult to be sanguine. The 'problem' is still seen as residing in the urban working classes and not in the problems that unjust structural relations present for these communities (Hills et al., 2009). This is compounded by the curriculum and pedagogy of a system that devalues and disregards what working-class children bring to school with them.

Urban education policies that situate the urban as a 'problem' and fail to build on alternative approaches to understanding the city (see Chapter 1) displace opportunities for different ways of 'doing' education. Urban education policies that continue (even indirectly) to support segregation and differentiation are not likely to foster socially just outcomes: 'The failure of education to produce benefits for people living in poverty is not simply a glitch in an otherwise benevolent system, but is a result of the inequalities built into society and the education system alike' (Raffo, 2009: 70).

In a period of economic turmoil, uncertainties and environmental crisis, there is a need for policy changes that move beyond the 'old' ways of doing things. There is a need to move away from a politics that once roused merely brings off small measures of redistribution within a policy discourse of 'blame' and 'deficit' that then seems to make very little longer term difference. What is needed is a policy that involves 'public decision aimed at *collective social improvement* from which *all* human lives should gain. That is the basis of progressive policy' (Hobsbawm, 2009: 33 *our italics*).

Further reading

Anyon, J. (2005) *Radical Possibilities: Public Policy, Urban Education, and a New Social Movement*. New York: Routledge.

Maguire, M. and Pratt-Adams, S. (2009) 'Improving the English Urban Primary School: Questions of Policy', *Improving Schools*, March, 12 (1): 1–12.

Maguire, M (2009) 'New Adulthood, Youth and Identity', in K. te Riele, (ed.) *Making Schools Different: Alternative Approaches to Educating Young People*. Sydney and London: Sage.

Useful websites

http://www.standards.dcsf.gov.uk/sie/si/SfCC/

Schools Facing Challenging Circumstances

http://www.uncommonschools.org/nsa/home/index.html

North Star Academy School – Newark, New Jersey

http://www.nfer.ac.uk/research-areas/education-policy/

National Foundation for Educational Research (NFER)

Part 3
Urban Education Policy into Practice

This part looks at three cases of urban policies in practice. By including a chapter on critical pedagogy, we demonstrate that there are alternative and socially just ways of working in urban educational settings that break with the way that education is currently being provided. We also look specifically at the Early Years setting, for this is foundational and has frequently been neglected by urban educationalists. Finally, we consider the potential of E-learning as a way of respecting the urban worlds of city learners and as a way of doing critical pedagogy.

Critical Urban Pedagogy

Introduction

Critical pedagogy is a teaching philosophy that has been developed in order to improve the educational experiences of marginalized and oppressed people; it is therefore explicitly political. In this chapter it is argued that critical pedagogy is crucial for urban school reform. It requires urban teachers to enter into a critical dialogue with students; designed to enable them to recognize and challenge unjust hierarchies of class, 'race' and gender. Two scholars who pioneered successful critical pedagogical practice are Paulo Freire and bell hooks. The first part of this chapter provides a reflective review of their thinking and practice, drawing on their substantive writings. The chapter then explores a number of urban case studies that illustrate how critical pedagogical practice can result in student success. Finally, arguments are made for developing critical pedagogy further within a range of urban settings.

Prior to examining Freire's and hooks' critical pedagogy, it may be helpful to clarify the usage of 'working class' and 'urban' in this chapter. Freire and hooks are concerned with developing a critical pedagogy that includes working-class students. Urban schools and settings educate working-class students, many of whom experience high levels of poverty and disadvantage (Maguire, Wooldridge and Pratt-Adams, 2006). Critical pedagogical practice may be of particular value for urban educators, since many poor working-class students continue to underachieve academically (Sparkes and Glennerster, 2002; Flaherty et al., 2004; Taylor, 2006).

Paulo Freire, reading the world as well as the word

Paulo Freire, who was born in Brazil in 1921 and died in 1997, has been described as one of the greatest educators of the twentieth century (Giroux, 1994; Gastaldo and de Figueiredo-Cowen, 1995). Throughout his life, Freire's teaching, educational writings and political campaigning were concerned with enabling the urban poor to carry out a 'reading of the world' as well as reading the word (Freire, 1998: 43). Freire demanded that students were offered a political education alongside an academic one. He believed that this progressive teaching was essential for freedom, in that students needed to reflect critically on the causes of their oppression (Freire, 1993). Freire was an urban teacher who inspired the world (Apple, 1990; Shor, 1992; Giroux, 1994). His radical educational philosophy was evidenced when he devised a 'method' for teaching adult literacy in Brazil in the early 1960s. Freire's innovative and highly successful methodology was used across Northern Brazil, until in 1964 a military coup jailed him for his 'subversive' work and he was subsequently exiled from his country of birth for 16 years (Gastaldo and de Figueiredo-Cowen, 1995; Freire, 1996). In exile, he taught, published and promoted literacy and education for critical consciousness, receiving honorary degrees from 29 universities in Europe and America. Freire returned to Brazil in 1980 and continued to lecture and refine his radical pedagogical theorizing. In 1989 he was appointed as Secretary of Education for the city of Sao Paulo.

The Pedagogy of the Oppressed

Freire's influential book, written while he was in exile, *The Pedagogy of the Oppressed*, was first published in the UK in 1970 and it outlines his original educational thinking and practice. It includes a critique of traditional teaching and argues for 'progressive' teaching that aims to enable all students to become 'critical co-investigators in dialogue with the teacher' (Freire, 1996: 62).

Freire argued that no education is neutral; as Foucault would later claim, in his analysis of the operation of social power, it is the most 'innocent' practices that are the most dangerous (Foucault, 1978). For example, the books the teacher selects not to use are as relevant as the ones that are selected. Freire's challenge of the neutrality of educational practice means that there needs to be a consideration of what education is for and whose social group interests are promoted. Teachers must critically reflect on their classroom pedagogy and understand how working-class students can be silenced in the classroom. Freire (1993: 59) condemns 'uncritical' educational practice: 'Education as the exercise of domination stimulates the credulity of students, with ideological intent (often not perceived by educators) of indoctrinating them to adapt to the world of oppression'. Not to examine the ideology inherent in practice is to allow the oppressors to continue to use education as a way of reinforcing their dominance.

In the same way as bankers 'deposit' money, Freire suggests that traditional pedagogical practice works to 'fill' the students with information that serves to maintain unjust hierarchies of power. Freire (1993: 58) describes the banking system in educational terms as follows:

> Based on a mechanistic, static, naturalistic, spatialized view of consciousness, it transforms students into receiving objects. It attempts to control thinking and action, leads women and men to adjust to the world, and inhibits their creative power.

Students are given no opportunity to critically discuss their thinking and what is taught. Working-class students come to believe the teacher's viewpoint. As Gramsci (1968) also argues, they accept the dominant hegemony that is designed to maintain the advantages of the ruling classes: 'In the banking concept of education, knowledge is a gift bestowed by those who consider themselves knowledgeable upon those whom they consider to know nothing' (Freire, 1993: 53).

In the banking system, poor working-class students are positioned as ignorant and less capable of independent thought by their teachers. Research has shown how these low-level expectations of students in urban schools continue and contribute to student underachievement (Giroux, 1992; hooks, 2000; Burn, 2001; Ball, 2003).

Freire writes with great respect for working-class students while acknowledging how the 'banking' system works to demoralize them and teach them they are unintelligent:

> So often do they hear that they are good for nothing, know nothing and are incapable of learning anything – that they are sick, lazy and unproductive – that in the end they become convinced of their own unfitness. (Freire, 1993: 45)

Freire spent his whole educational life challenging this deficit 'banking' system and exploring how 'critical dialogue' enables working-class students to become powerful in their own learning.

The progressive teacher is central to Freire's vision. Through critical dialogue the teacher and the student both become active in their learning. Freire (1993: 71) argues that this joint intellectual activity requires teachers to have 'humility' and not see themselves as the keepers of the knowledge to 'bestow' on the ignorant students, but rather through 'dialogue, the teacher-of-the-students and the students-of-the-teacher cease to exist and a new term emerges: teacher-student with student-teachers' (Freire, 1993: 61).

This shift of power positions the teacher and student as co-investigators and the students are provoked, through problem-posing, to develop and justify their thinking and analysis of social power. Freire makes clear that the vision of the teacher must not stifle the vision of the students. As the students develop their critical thinking they come to see that transformation is possible. Acceptance of external circumstances is replaced by the recognition that they can challenge inequalities. In this way teaching becomes liberating and education itself the practice of freedom:

> In problem-posing education, people develop their power to perceive critically the way they exist in the world with which and in which they find themselves; they come to see the world not as a static reality, but as a reality in progress, in transformation. (Freire, 1993: 64)

It is a pedagogy that identifies critical dialogue between students and teacher as essential for students to 'create history and become historical human beings' (Freire, 1993: 82). He believes critical pedagogy is an act of love, a love that is not 'sentimental' but rather 'an act of freedom' that requires a love of the world. In dialogic teaching, the reading of the word becomes also the reading of the world, in order to transform it.

While denouncing the 'banking' system of education, Freire accepts that many teachers who carry out this oppressive form of pedagogy may be unaware of its effects: 'there are innumerable well-intentioned bank-clerk teachers who do not realize that they are serving only to dehumanize' (Freire, 1993: 56). Freire claimed that students as well as teachers needed to be active in their learning. He devised culture circles as a form of critical pedagogy for teaching adult literacy. They developed from his identification that students as well as teachers need to be active subjects in their learning.

Adult students, in circles of no more than 20, have ownership of the curriculum, in that they identify 'generative themes' for critical investigation. These culture circles can be set up wherever is convenient, including barns or local halls. The circle may also include a sociologist and psychologist alongside a teacher, providing a multidisciplinary team who will take notes and sometimes tape record the dialogue that develops as the theme is critically discussed by the group. In accordance with Freire's vision of teacher/students as co-investigators, once the themes have been identified by the students, the coordinators will further scrutinize the themes. They will listen to tapes, reflect on the notes taken and offer further 'hinged themes' to extend the opportunities for problem-posing and critical dialogue to occur within the culture circle. This ongoing process with continual evaluation by the team will lead to the coordinators (with local assistants drawn from the group) developing appropriate teaching materials. Educators

> must never provide the people with programs which have little or nothing to do with their own preoccupations, doubts, hopes and fears . . . It is not our role to speak to the people about our own view of the world, nor to attempt to impose that view on them, but rather dialogue with the people about their view and ours. (Freire, 1993: 77)

Teaching materials will be drawn from the students' environment and may include photographs, slides, posters, taped interviews and newspaper articles; and they will inform the subsequent development of oral, written and political literacy. In this way each specific urban setting can form a relevant context for both academic and political study. The final choice of resources will be informed by the investigation of the evolving themes. One example Freire provides is when an 'expert' in the selected theme is interviewed on tape and his/her photograph taken. The taped interview is then played to the culture circle and a relevant introduction provided while the photograph is projected onto the screen. The culture circle will critically discuss the interview and the expert will be offered feedback from the group. Freire (1993: 103) discusses how 'This technique links intellectuals, often well-intentioned but not infrequently alienated from the reality of the people, to that reality. It also gives people an opportunity to hear and criticize the thought of intellectuals.'

Finally, once all the teaching materials are ready, the teams of educators, who may have also prepared introductory manuals, re-present the 'themes':

> The people will find themselves in this program; it will not seem strange to them, since it originated with them. The educator will also explain (based on the dialogical character of education) the presence in the program of the hinged themes, and their significance. (Freire, 1993: 104)

Out of ongoing critical dialogue, concerning a theme selected by the students, materials are generated by both the students and educators; these are subsequently used as building blocks for literacy work that is meaningful to all of the students and their cultures. Within these culture circles the development of literacy becomes the development of 'real consciousness of the world' (Freire, 1993: 96). By naming the world, working-class students can become active subjects who are able to understand and therefore challenge their oppression. Freire's culture circles have inspired urban educators across the world (O'Malley, 1997) in that they have enabled teachers of the poor to recognize that students themselves have cultural knowledge that can form the basis of a problem-solving critical pedagogy.

Skeggs (1997: 20) argued that theories 'always bear the marks of their makers'. Freire in his later writings reflects on how in his early life he lived alongside slum children, after his family was forced to leave their middle-class home for political reasons. He learnt how poverty and hunger impact on student learning, including his own (Freire, 1996). He also started to explore how working-class families can internalize negative beliefs about themselves, accepting that they are 'inferior' to the middle and upper classes (Freire, 1993: 45). Gastaldo and de Figueiredo-Cowen (1995) argue that an examination of Freire's own life experience serves to illuminate his ground-breaking theorizing. However, Freire recognized that not all oppressed people continue to value their own community once they have achieved; in this case the oppressed become the oppressors.

Freire returned to Brazil in 1979 and continued to interrogate his reflective practice. He was interested in how technology and globalization were impacting on pedagogy (see Chapter 9). Freire argued that these new challenges must be critically examined for their potential to support urban school reform (Freire, 1998). For instance, the internet allows students global access to examining and debating a wide range of educational beliefs and practices. Communication and uncensored internet-based research possibilities provide increased access to students, especially those studying part-time or with childcare responsibilities that require them to be home-based. The possibilities of technology to support urban education as the practice of freedom are being increasingly realized.

Activity

How realistic would it be to adopt culture circles in urban schools?

---

bell hooks, teaching to transgress

bell hooks is an African-American Professor of English at City College in New York. She is the author of many books concerned with feminism, racism and pedagogy; describing herself as 'a feminist theorist and social critic' (hooks, 1994: 52). She uses the pseudonym bell hooks, with lower case initials, in order to acknowledge an older relative who was criticized for answering back by her family and community because she would not fulfil the stereotyped female role; and in her own writing hooks is determined not to be silenced (hooks, 1989). hooks acknowledges how much of an influence Paulo Freire's thinking has been on her own pedagogical practice within university classrooms. In the 1960s hooks entered higher education, as a student from a black working-class background, and experienced racism, sexism and class bias. She looked for a way of both understanding and resisting the exclusionary practices she was subject to (hooks, 2000). When hooks read Freire, she:

> . . . deeply identified with the marginalised peasants he speaks about, or with my black brothers and sisters, my comrades in Guinea-Bissau. You see I was coming from a rural southern black experience, into the university, and I had lived through the struggle for racial desegregation and was in resistance without

having a political language to articulate that process. Paulo was one of the thinkers whose work gave me a language. (hooks, 1994: 46)

In her early all-black schooling, hooks had experience of 'the transformative power of teaching, of pedagogy' (hooks, 1989: 50). Her female black teachers were affirmative and political; they employed a wide range of challenging teaching strategies, enabling hooks and her classmates to achieve their academic potentials, despite sexism and racism. hooks refers to these urban teachers as her 'pedagogical guardians' (hooks, 1989: 50). In Freire's terms, they taught her to read the world as well as the text. The contrast between this critical practice and the 'banking' system hooks then endured in integrated schools and at university was stark. As an undergraduate at Stanford University, hooks found professors who lectured on challenging oppression engaging in repressive classroom practices which silenced and marginalized students like herself. A student of English, she studied works written, in the main, by white males from advantaged backgrounds and began to doubt her ability to survive in such an alien environment. hooks (1994) describes her time at Stanford as akin to a prison sentence. Remembering the excitement of the classrooms created by the inspired black teachers of her early schooling, hooks searched for a different way of theorizing learning and teaching. 'When I discovered the work of the Brazilian thinker Paulo Freire, my first introduction to critical pedagogy, I found a mentor and a guide, someone who understood that learning could be liberatory' (hooks, 1994: 6).

hooks also explored anti-colonial and feminist pedagogies, determined to 'read' and therefore resist oppression; these powerful formative experiences framed hooks' subsequent teaching and theorizing within the academy. Once she started teaching in university, hooks was determined not to replicate the pedagogical practices she had endured as an undergraduate.

Activity

Think about any experiences you have had where the teaching style and/or curriculum offered was not supportive of your learning.

How could changes have been made to enable you to be more fully involved in your learning?

In *Teaching to Transgress* (1994) hooks reflects on how, over time, she developed feminist critical pedagogy within university classrooms. In this book she devotes a chapter to an 'imagined' conversation about Freire: examining the need to refine Freire's theorizing in order to challenge the inherent sexism in his early writings and develop critical pedagogical strategies for education in multicultural urban classrooms. hooks argues that the act of teaching must be recognized as a key way of challenging or reinforcing social injustices (see also Raphael Reed, 1995). She considers that 'pedagogy' itself is often undervalued and not seen as worthy of serious study, a criticism also made in the UK (Alexander, 2004). hooks' writing is based on many years of teaching and theorizing on 'race', class and gender; practices which still work to exclude many poor working-class students within urban classrooms (Gillborn and Mirza, 2000).

For example, Osler and Vincent (2003) researched 81 vulnerable teenage girls attending UK urban schools. They reported how, in one multicultural school, the girls and their parents 'felt that the curriculum did not address their everyday realities. They perceived the curriculum to be narrow and largely monocultural' (Osler and Vincent, 2003: 128). Research by Connolly (1998) in another UK urban school found that racism and sexism worked alongside class to lower the educational achievement of a group of young boys. Gilborn and Mirza (2000) and Blair (2001) have also documented further examples of how class, 'race' and gender practices can impact on the educational achievements of poor working-class students in urban schools.

Feminist critical pedagogy

Feminists have criticized some approaches to critical pedagogy for ignoring gender and patriarchy (Luke and Gore, 1992). In his meeting with hooks, Freire acknowledged the sexism in his early writings and the need for sexism and other injustices to be challenged (hooks, 1994). Even so, hooks found Freire's writings spoke to her as a working-class black woman, far more than the mainstream feminist texts which were focused on the lives of white advantaged women. She has since 'taken threads of Paulo's work and woven it into that version of feminist pedagogy I believe my work as writer and teacher embodies' (hooks, 1994: 52). hooks' version of feminist pedagogy demands that students and teachers examine and challenge sexism alongside racism and class bias. She defines feminism as 'a movement to end sexist oppression' and recognizes 'the inter-relatedness of sex, race and class oppression' (hooks, 1984: 31). hooks (2000) argues that institutional bias against working-class black and white students is often ignored (see also Skeggs, 1997). In her influential book *Feminist Theory: From Margin to Center*, hooks criticizes white middle-class feminists for ignoring racism and class bias; she also argues that men must become involved in challenging sexism, as we are all enmeshed in these power relations (hooks, 1984).

hooks emphasizes the emotionality of teaching and learning, acknowledging the problematic nature of engaging in feminist critical pedagogy. She argues that teachers and students must learn to accept different ways of knowing. Working-class students, especially those from different ethnic groups, may have very different knowledges and these differences need to be drawn on; this can at times be challenging. She suggests that it is important that the urban teacher receives critical feedback, rather than instant 'love':

> The exciting aspect of creating a classroom community where there is respect for individual voices is that there is infinitely more feedback because students do feel free to talk – and talk back. And, yes, often this feedback is critical. Moving away from the need for immediate affirmation was crucial to my growth as a teacher. (hooks, 1994: 42)

In her writings about feminist critical pedagogy, hooks openly describes feelings of love and hate; she refuses to be bound by the traditional mind/body split and discusses 'pedagogical strategies that may be not just for our students but for ourselves' (hooks, 1994: 134). In this practice she constructs teaching as transformative for herself as well as for students and thus avoids what she sees as the false face of 'neutrality' that Freire had condemned in the banking system (Freire, 1993).

Another 'thread' hooks has drawn on from Freire's educational writings concerns the need for theory and practice. hooks condemns the devaluing of intellectual development:

> Bourgeois class biases have led many feminist theorists to develop ideas that have little or no relation to the lived experiences of most women . . . Annoyed and angered by these ideas, many women dismiss all theory as irrelevant. Yet women need to know that ideas and theories are important. (hooks, 1984: 112)

hooks calls for rigorous engagement in theorizing and the importance of relating the sharing of lived experience to academic subject matter. In this model the teacher is always scaffolding serious respectful dialogue and thinking. However, this dialogue must be focused. In one example, hooks describes how she will interrupt a student and say 'that's interesting, but how does that relate to the novel we're reading?' (hooks, 1994: 151). At no time does the teacher abdicate her/his responsibility to provoke shared intellectual development. She positions herself and her students as 'workers' in the classroom, involved in the creation of a dynamic learning community. Students have a right to speak, a responsibility to listen, contribute to critical discussions and to respect difference. Teaching and learning are hard work but it can also be exciting and pleasurable, especially when there are opportunities to draw on a wider range of cultural knowledges – often a feature of urban classrooms.

hooks argues that teachers as well as students must become 'self-actualized' and should have periods away from teaching in order to refresh and renew their passion for pedagogy (1994: 165). In her writings she affirms the university classroom as 'the most radical space of possibility' while recognizing that each learning community will be unique and teaching strategies must be constantly refined and changed by the participants, rather than following a static blueprint (hooks, 1994: 12).

Ecclestone (2004) suggests that the critical pedagogical visions of Freire's and hooks' have sometimes been misunderstood and employed in a way that reaffirms the banking system.

Critical pedagogy in urban settings

The critical urban pedagogy Freire pioneered is a practical philosophy that has been usefully applied in a wide range of educational contexts. In this section, we offer four examples of innovative urban critical pedagogy, in Primary, Secondary, and Adult Education settings. Although the context and subject matter vary, all of the examples provided position the students as 'critical co-investigators' (Freire, 1996: 62).

Inspired by Freire's pedagogy, an evening adult learning project in Edinburgh was set up to investigate 'social and cultural issues affecting Scottish people' (O'Malley, 1997: 4). At the start, 50 working-class students, many of whom had left school with few qualifications, were given cameras to record their community life. They subsequently met in focus groups to discuss the meanings of the photographs and the issues identified by members of their community. Collectively, the students and the tutors then devised curriculum study groups based on common interests, such as democracy, women's history, the stories of local families and buildings. For instance, one group used libraries and old newspapers to explore how the tenements had originally been built for industrial workers during times of industrial affluence. This history class was run on Freirean lines, though the adults decided to go further and voted to have no tutor; instead they organized their research strategies and prepared presentations for the rest of the class. The ownership of the learning and the exploring of their own cultural traditions allowed these working-class people to reclaim their voices and community, organizing social and political events, as well as continuing to develop their literacy in meaningful contexts. There are now over 500 registered members who continue the educational and political work, one of them, Rona discusses how: 'I wisnae used tae being listened to anywhere. To be shown that what ye know, what ye think, what you are saying is of value – I hadnae experienced that before' (cited in O'Malley, 1997: 5).

Freire saw pedagogy as 'a cultural and political practice that takes place not only in schools but in all cultural spheres' (Giroux, 1994: 146). This Scottish Adult Education class demonstrates the possibilities of this practice. It reaffirms Freire's belief that people who have been failed by a banking system can become active agents in their learning if the pedagogic practice places students' cultural traditions and knowledges as legitimate parts of a co-constructed critical problem-solving curriculum.

In the following example of urban practice, student interest in hip-hop music and the spoken word are employed as a way of developing education for social justice. Stovall (2006: 63) reports on how four 'poetry educators', working in a range of urban settings, are developing a culturally relevant pedagogy for young people in Chicago. The four poets are all rooted in oral and literacy traditions; they have performed on a cable TV programme popular with the adolescents they teach; they represent the cultural diversity of the economically poor community they work in; they see poetry, hip-hop and soul music as legitimate materials with which young people can critically engage, as they are features of their own culture. Rather than ignoring the expert knowledge these students have of popular music and dance, these can be valuable resources for critical examination. For example, the misogyny in some of the popular music can be challenged and regular poetry 'slams' are held, together with open microphone sessions. In poetry slams the performers compete in front of audiences who vote for their favourite performance. Workshops take place in detention centres, schools and community centres. Stovall (2006: 64), who researched these projects, argues that teaching social justice through poetics can provoke young people to 'develop understandings of their world and begin to engage the world as agents of change'. This is a central tenet of Freire's education for critical consciousness (Freire, 1993) which links learning to social transformation. The young people are required to listen to other voices as well as speak their own; it is not a programme to produce 'poets' but to gain knowledge of other cultures and to enable the students to celebrate their own oral and written traditions.

Stovall (2006) believes that, in many mainstream urban schools, the Arts have been marginalized and young working-class students may not have access to creative spaces. Stovall suggests that it is within these challenging poetry and music sessions that critical pedagogy can flourish. However, he also points out how financially vulnerable these urban poetic sessions are in 'an age where test scores are argued to be the sole determinant of academic achievement' (Stovall, 2006: 79).

Activity

What would a culturally relevant pedagogy look like in an urban school?

Another example demonstrates how innovative pedagogy can be seen merely as an 'add-on' rather than a legitimate way of educating. In England one mathematics project 'CAN', set up to explore the usage of calculators, had substantial success in a number of Primary Schools (Rousham, 1995). This project gave calculators to seven-year olds and invited classroom teachers and families to become involved in their young children's mathematical learning. One of the classroom teachers, working in an urban school with over 90 per cent of students on free school meals, has written about how this project allowed her working-class students and their families to become successfully engaged with learning in a way that challenged class bias (Burn, 2000a).

Mathematics is a school subject that has long been presented as 'neutral'; however, as Wright (1992) has shown in her research, and Freire argues, the myth of 'neutrality' continues to mask gender, class and 'race' bias. The maths research project required Burn and the other class teachers involved not to 'teach' traditional sums but to allow the students to explore calculators and adopt a problem-solving pedagogical approach. The children dialogued with each other, their families and the teachers in order to explain and justify their mathematical thinking; the teacher's role was to provoke and challenge them further. The children and their families set the agenda, recording in their own informal ways when necessary (Burn, 2000a). No longer was the class teacher the 'keeper' of the mathematical knowledge to be 'deposited' as Freire described in his analysis of the oppressive banking system, instead they became subjects in their own learning (Freire, 1993). Burn (2000a: 3) reports: 'The constant "numerical dialogue" engendered between the pupils and ourselves, as teachers, led to high challenge and refinement of strategies used by ALL pupils, including girls.'

Burn (2000a) highlighted the support that classroom teachers, like herself, were offered from university researchers; both practice and theory were essential components of this project, a combination Freire insisted was vital (Freire, 1996). Despite the positive results, the introduction of a National Curriculum meant the potential of this small mathematical project was never fully developed (Rousham, 1995).

Another example of critical urban pedagogy that involves practice and research is based on teaching English literature to Secondary School students in a Northern California urban centre. Duncan-Andrade and Morrell (2007) set out to develop and theorize a critical pedagogy approach in their teaching of literature. The teachers followed Freire's approach and invited the working-class students to critically examine both 'popular' and 'high culture' texts, looking for cultural bias. In this way they deconstructed Shakespeare and hip-hop, arguing that 'literacy educators can encourage a critical multicultural reading of any text' (Duncan-Andrade and Morrell, 2007: 186). The students were encouraged to examine texts such as national legislation and mortgage offers, reflecting on their power to exclude; in short they were becoming critically literate and able to challenge taken-for-granted cultural practices. Films were viewed and carefully deconstructed to examine how 'race', gender, class and sexuality were represented. These literacy activities were challenging and required the students to carry out extensive research, engage in critical debate, prepare presentations and 'take ownership over the knowledge production process' (Duncan-Andrade and Morrell, 2007: 188).

The teachers in this study discussed how schools for the urban poor continue to be under-resourced and disadvantaged. In their own particular classroom, the physical environment itself was poor, with no heating and very limited access to computers. They found that as the students became more able to 'read' the world, they also started to challenge the conditions in which they were expected to study and they used their political knowledge to gain local media attention. Duncan-Andrade and Morrell (2007) report how some teachers and administrators opposed this action and tensions arose between fighting for social justice and overcoming prejudice from non-supportive colleagues. They also received negative comments from people who continued to view working-class urban students as deficit and as incapable of academic thinking (Skeggs, 1997; Burn, 2001; Byrne, 2005). This example demonstrates that critical urban pedagogy can be legislated against and subject to censure and opposition by powerful others.

Conclusion

In reviewing Freire's work and hooks' subsequent adaptation of his pedagogical approach, this chapter asserts that critical pedagogy practice, as developed by Freire and hooks, remains relevant for teachers and students in a wide range of contemporary urban settings. However, the education marketplace continues to label urban schools and their working-class students as 'failing and deficient' (Apple, 2006b; Giroux, 2009). Currently, all teachers, including urban teachers, are working within the increasing restraints of externally imposed assessment, which Kohl (1998: 44), an experienced urban teacher, argues is a central barrier to successful teaching:

> It is very difficult for a teacher, in the context of evaluation-obsessed and product-oriented schools and universities, to teach well if teaching well includes creating intimate, personal, and thorough engagement with content . . . This is as true in kindergarten, the middle grades, and high school as it is in college.

However, the examples of critical urban pedagogy provided in this chapter illustrate the potential for innovative practice, successful students and engaged teachers. Teaching is lived as a passionate and political intellectual act (hooks, 1994). Teachers, as well as the students they teach, are involved in self-actualization; they are reading the world as well as the word. Freire (1995: 18) believes that education involves 'utopias, dreams, desires and values' and critical pedagogy aims to allow all students, regardless of their background, to become powerful in their own learning.

Further reading

Apple, M., Au, W. and Gandin, L. A. (eds) (2009) *The Routledge International Handbook of Critical Education*. New York; London: Routledge.

Compton-Lilly, C. (ed.) (2009) *Breaking the Silence: Recognizing the Social and Cultural Resources Students Bring to the Classroom.* Newark, DE: International Reading Association.

Davidson, M., del G. and Yancy, G. (eds) (2009) *Critical Perspectives on bell hooks.* New York, NY: Routledge.

Groenke, S. L. and Amos Hatch, J. (eds) (2009) *Critical Pedagogy and Teacher Education in the Neoliberal Era: Small Openings.* Dordrecht: Springer.

Useful websites

http://mingo.info-science.uiowa.edu/~stevens/critped/page1.htm

Critical Pedagogy on the Web

http://www.freireproject.org/category/topic-tags/paulo-freire-critical-pedagogy-social-justice

The Freire project

http://www.ernestmorrell.com/criticalpedagogy

This website provides further examples of critical urban pedagogy

Early Years Education in the Urban Context 8

Chapter Outline

Introduction

In this chapter, we explore some of the key policy and practice issues in the provision of education and care for the very young urban child. The reason why Early Years education is so important, perhaps the *most* important area for historical and sociological inquiry, is that it is the foundational stage. This is the 'moment' when families and the education state are formally brought together. It is the 'moment' when judgements are made about different families, their values, attitudes and aspirations. Thus, it is not surprising that it is a key area for intervention and action. Writing of Early Years provision in the US, O'Connell Rust (2003: 155) says that two dominant discourses have continued to shape provision. These suggest that

> the child is 'at risk' and therefore in need of saving so that the society as a whole will be able to sustain itself economically and socially; in the other view, the child is a resource whose rightful support and education will shape the society of the future.

She adds that 'the first view has largely shaped policies directed toward children of poverty'.

In the UK, Melhuish (2004) has provided a succinct account of the need for Early Years provision, highlighting the needs of children and parents and relating these to economic imperatives. It is worth quoting what he says at length to illustrate his argument:

> There are 2.9 million children in England below compulsory school age. Early childhood is a crucial period for human development and can shape the remainder of people's lives. It is, therefore, a time when children need high quality care and educational experiences. Evidence suggests *this is particularly the case for those from currently disadvantaged groups* such as children with special educational needs or from ethnic minorities. Early Years provision, including childcare and pre-school education, is thus aimed at supporting children's learning and development and is also *a key element of the Government welfare to work policies*. The Government has given priority to services for disadvantaged groups in particular, in order to tackle social exclusion. (Mclhurish, 2004; our italics)

This chapter starts with a brief discussion of what is encompassed by the term 'Early Years'. Then it reviews the historical development of Early Years provision in urban settings, identifying key discourses that were, and still are, utilized to construct young working-class children as in need of 'care and control'. It also highlights other key discourses that have continued to shape the provision for Early Years education, such as welfare to work (see Melhuish 2004, cited above). Drawing on some qualitative data collected in a set of small-scale illuminative studies (Burn, 2000b; 2001; 2005a), the chapter briefly examines the perspectives of a number of present-day urban Early Years teachers in order to highlight some of the stereotyping that continues to 'other' working-class children at this early stage of their schooling. Finally, some recent government interventions such as Sure Start and the Early Years

Foundation Stage Curriculum are considered and the move towards more equitable urban educational practice is discussed.

What is Early Years education?

In the UK, Early Years generally refers to the provision being made for children aged five years and under. However, this description includes a swathe of alternative provisions such as registered child-minders, nannies, parent and toddler groups, playgroups, crèches, state and private nurseries and the Reception Classes in Primary Schools for 5-year olds. It also includes Children Centres and Sure Start providers catering for 0- to 5-year-olds in designated areas of 'deprivation'. There is also a range of differently educated and trained workers in Early Years provision (Osborne, 2006). For example, Early Years teachers have generally been trained to teach children between the ages of 3 to 7 years. However, in England, the Early Years Curriculum (DCSF, 2008) now applies to children from birth to the age of five including those being child-minded or attending nurseries, Children Centres and state Infant or Primary Schools. Those state professionals who are currently being trained and prepared to work in these settings, some with Early Years Professional Status (EYPS) and others who have different qualifications and training, such as nursery nurses, will work in the three Early Years age groups identified by the UK government as babies (0–20 months), toddlers (16–36 months) and young children (30–60 months). Overall, the provision for children under five, the non-statutory sector, is piecemeal, patchy and internally differentiated. What is available will vary according to location and costs. So, in urban settings while there may be more provision, charges will vary enormously; in other areas there may just be a parent and toddler group in the local hall available for a few hours each day.

Historical overview of Early Years provision

Early childcare provision in the nineteenth century was driven by sometimes conflicting concerns such as attempting to keep mothers at home and out of the workplace as well as fears about potentially unruly children. Then as now, powerful discourses about the importance of the mother in their children's early socialization and development were paramount. However, in the industrializing cities, where poverty and deprivation were widespread, many working-class mothers were forced to take up paid employment in order to support their families. As Baldock et al. (2005: 161) describe,

> poor quality, entirely unofficial care of children by women known as 'baby farmers' spread in the industrial cities. Reformers at the end of the nineteenth century and beginning of the next set up pioneering efforts in nursery education and the provision of outdoor play for the children of the slums.

The first Infant School in the UK was opened by a factory owner in New Lanark, Scotland in 1816. Robert Owen, a radical socialist, opened his school for the workers' children aged from one upwards in his 'model' town of New Lanark. Hall (1995: 137) suggests that Owen's actions were built on 'a commitment to love'. The curriculum was designed to encourage spontaneous play, outside play and regular outings (Peltzman, 1998). In contrast Sanderson (1983: 52) suggests that Owen's Infant School was set up to 'save' these young children from 'the influence of their parents'. Owen's ideas were influential and by 1819 one of his teachers, James Buchanan, had moved from New Lanark to London where he joined with others to form the London Infant School Society. This Society, led by middle-class men, was established in 1825 for the education of young working-class children (Clarke, 1985). At this time, Victorian middle-class men were positioning themselves as public guardians and educators of young, vulnerable working-class children. Samuel Wilderspin was the leader of this Infant School Movement and he believed men were best suited for running Infant Schools as they would 'exercise a greater degree of authority over children' (McCann and Young, 1982: 175). Men were developing 'nurseries for the body and soul', ensuring that the social order was safeguarded (Martin and Goodman, 2004: 64). Sutherland (1971) argues that this Infant School Movement was a 'moral mission' set up to ensure that social class hierarchies were maintained. These Infant Schools set out to teach 'obedience, cheerful subordination, cleanliness' (Clarke, 1985: 79). Sutherland (1971) and Clarke (1985) claim that the early schooling provided for the children of the urban poor was concerned with social engineering alongside basic education. In order to be effective, this work of 'redemption' and 'correction' had to start as early as possible.

All educational provision is premised on a set of beliefs and values. In the urban settings of the nineteenth century, powerful discourses operated to construct poor children as needing to be 'corrected' and 'educated' into acceptable behaviour (Brehony, 2000). Early pioneering educators were convinced that in order to establish and maintain a 'certain' type of society, the children of the poor needed to be tamed and 'educated' to accept its doctrine as soon as possible. 'The children of the labouring poor were to be taught to stay in their places without being a burden to society; they were bound to their betters by ties of gratitude' (Sutherland, 1971: 5).

At the same time that men like Owen, Buchanan and Wilderspin were opening Infant Schools, other groups were also attempting to 'save' the children of the urban poor. There was an escalating demand for cheap child labour in the emerging factories of the industrializing cities. On Sundays, their day off, their 'wild and mischievous behaviour' needed curbing (Curtis, 1967: 197). The Sunday School movement had been set up by Robert Raikes in the 1780s, and families were charged a penny for their children to attend these schools. Fears of social unrest and revolution also contributed to the development of Early Years and Elementary schooling for the growing numbers of poor children (Sutherland, 1971; Goldstrom, 1972). A range of factory and 'ragged' schools were opened during this period of industrial growth, a time when many young children (and their families) endured terrible poverty. All of this piecemeal provision for the children of the urban poor helped cement the belief that these young children were in need of moral instruction as much if not more than an academic education. Working-class parenting was seen as inadequate and in need of remediation (Harris, 1993).

The beginning of official state involvement in educating the poor was legislated for through the Health and Morals Apprentices Act in 1802. This legislation demanded that employers took responsibility for the education of their child-workers (Sutherland, 1971). At this stage, discourses of social control underpinned this fairly meagre provision. Education was 'seen as the solution to the social and political threat to the ruling class posed by the concentration of large numbers of working-class people in the rapidly expanding cities of the early nineteenth century' (Clarke, 1985: 74).

While the provision for Early Years schooling was dominated by the leadership of males and discourses of control and discipline, gradually these were augmented by alternative discourses that started to construct Early Years provision as a maternal mission. The control element persisted, but in different guises. Walkerdine (1992) argues that the shift towards female-only teachers in the later part of the nineteenth century was based on a belief that the young children of the urban poor could be 'saved' by love. In consequence, Froebelian approaches to Early Years education in England were sponsored by a group of middle-class women who developed discourses of 'spiritual motherhood' in order to enable them to enter the public sphere as teachers (Brehony, 2000:186). Froebel had argued that the 'teaching of young children was, ideally, the mother made conscious' and middle-class Victorian women increasingly claimed Early Years teaching as their 'maternal' right and duty (Moriarty, 1998: 1). By the end of the nineteenth century, Early Years teaching was a female-only occupation.

Harris (1993) suggests that during this time 'good' mothering was increasingly seen as contributing towards the welfare of the Nation and Empire. The children of the poor would now be 'mothered' by female middle-class teachers into becoming compliant citizens who would accept their place in the social hierarchy and respect their betters (Sutherland, 1971). Thus, the origins of Early Years education is a story of the schooling of the urban poor set against concerns about their alleged inadequate parenting. That this occurred in a period when national growth and prosperity (for some) depended on the paid labour of these working-class mothers and their young children is also a key part of this story. 'The education of working class children was presented as their rescue from the abyss' (Davin, 1996: 134).

Activity

What policies and provisions can you identify that support the idea that urban working-class families are still seen as 'deficit' and in need of 'rescue'?

Continuities in Early Years provision

One of the major continuities between the Early Years provision of the early twentieth and twenty-first centuries is that Early Years teaching is still predominantly a feminized division of labour. Many of the women who work in various occupations within the Early Years setting have not always been formally qualified (child-minders, nursery assistants), thus, there has been a tendency to see this work as unskilled and low-status (Reay, 2001). Nicholson et al. (2008) have argued that the employment of many unqualified women in Children Centres and other urban childcare settings reaffirms the belief that Early Years provision needs to offer substitute 'mothering' rather than intellectual challenge. Cameron et al. (1999: 165) have argued that 'Early childhood services have to a greater or lesser extent been seen as offering mother substitutes'. In urban settings, this would mean 'mothering' the 'children of the poor' (Walkerdine and Lucey, 1989; Cunningham, 2000).

A second example of continuity across the centuries of Early Years provision relates to issues of class and the demonization of working-class children and their families. As Walkerdine (1992: 18) has claimed, Early Years teachers are still expected to 'provide a quasi-maternal nurturance to compensate for the depraved environments of the poor'. Since New Labour came to power in the UK in 1997, concerns about childhood poverty have been moved to the centre of policy-making. However, alongside these undoubted concerns with alleviating poverty run parallel concerns about order, control and alleged social 'breakdown'. Urban poverty is once again seen as a threat to social cohesion and early childhood poverty remains a key indicator of later educational failure (Flaherty et al., 2004; Howard, 2004).

These two continuities of classed and gendered discourses do not stand separately from one another. In practice, they are interwoven and overlapping. Thus, the mantle of motherhood bestowed onto well-meaning women teachers can easily mask a social engineering intent of state intervention for the youngest children of the poor – whose cultural practices may still be considered 'abnormal' compared to those of young middle-class children in our urban schools and settings (Walkerdine et al., 2001: 120). In some cases, seemingly 'innocent' and benevolent maternal discourses may well be effective in both de-politicizing and devaluing any more radical forms of Early Years education (Thornton and Brunton, 2009).

Activity

What do you think about all the television programmes that aim at teaching parents how to parent? What sorts of families are involved in these programmes?

Other discourses have played a part in the construction and provision of Early Years education and care. Moss (2003) claims that a belief in maternal care at home as the best provision for young children has had an enduring part to play. He argues, for instance, that during the Second World War the state opened many day nurseries so that mothers could go out to work while men were being posted overseas. Once the war was over, the majority of these nurseries were closed. Even in 1967, the Plowden Report was still arguing for part-time nurseries because 'they discouraged mothers from working and children needed to be with their mothers, at least part of the day' (Baldcock et al., 2005: 47). Moss (2003) also claims that the gendered division of labour has played a pivotal role in shaping provision of Early Years provision. Female expectations of a career as well as motherhood, combined with changes in the labour market (more work available for women), have provoked a demand for more childcare outside the family. Moss recognizes that national economic survival has also played a part in driving the demand for Early Years provision. Childcare provision encourages low-income families (mothers) into employment; this enhanced income helps in the battle against poverty as well as ensuring that there is a steady stream of women available for part-time, low-paid service sector employment that 'fits' with their family responsibilities.

One of the challenges in writing about Early Years policy and urban education concerns is that inevitably it is hard to tease out and isolate these matters: 'often the aims of policy are multi-layered and complex, interweaving Early Years developments with other linked goals' (Baldcock et al., 2005: 39). The UK government has recognized that 'our economy will prosper if more skilled and capable people are able to take up job opportunities because they have access to good quality, affordable and accessible childcare' (DfES, 1997: 7). Finding acceptable and affordable childcare before and to supplement the hours of statutory school provision presents emotional and practical difficulties for many parents. However, critical discourses alleging that maternal care in the home is best have never been allowed to interrupt the early childcare arrangements of the wealthy who have always relied upon legions of paid help (frequently working-class mothers) who have tended to their homes and supported their childcare. While the gender discourses of women taking the lead responsibility for child-care have not diminished, when these are aligned to other aspects of identity, 'many working class and black and minority ethnic families, prefer informal care' as opposed to highly regulated more formal arrangements (Ball and Vincent, 2005: 202). What parents want is not necessarily a 'one size fits all' approach towards Early Years provision. However, legislation in this area may be less concerned with what parents want, or what children might need, and more about societal and economic requirements.

In terms of Early Years provision and urban families however, the policy argument for state intervention has been justified through concerns to reduce childhood poverty and 'interrupt' the alleged underachievement of children growing up in poverty. These concerns have led to various provisions 'to support children and families in their earliest years of life to combat multiple disadvantages that had a significant negative influence on children's life chances' (Baldcock et al., 2005: 43). These provisions have not been intended for families that are more affluent. In these approaches, the families of the urban poor are seen as struggling and perhaps failing, and thus in need of direct intervention. To this extent, a pattern of state professional intervention, from services set up to 'rescue' and 'save' as well as 'educate parents', has been built up. Children in need of being 'saved' from the worse excesses of their families need to be reached out to as early as possible. The difference over time is that, in the past, state professionals were frequently middle-class experts who imposed their perceptions of 'good parenting' onto their 'clients' – the children and their parents of the urban poor. Currently, the intention is to work collaboratively in partnership with families in ways that empower and strengthen families and communities (Swick, 2003). Underlying this provision and intervention is an enduring discourse where some families are positioned as in distress, and as dysfunctional and difficult; these are the families of the working-class urban child.

The experiences of (some) urban Early Years teachers

However, there are other discourses that see the urban child and the urban family in somewhat different ways. Grace (2007: 971) has argued that education workers in urbanized settings have a 'very good understanding of the complex of social forces working against the schools and they have intelligent suggestions for policy and action to assist the schools'. However, their voices are frequently marginalized. If they ask for additional resources, they are seen as having a 'vested interest'; if they are being critical, they are seen as being too 'political'. The end result, as Grace (2007: 971) acknowledges, is that 'those who know the most . . . are inhibited from expressing these (views) publicly'. Instead, as Grace (2007: 971) argues, 'those who know least', media pundits and the constantly revolving set of government ministers 'achieve maximum publicity for their accounts'.

One of the most enduring findings is that achievement in school is correlated to social background. Research shows that by the age of five, working-class children are already achieving less than their middle-class peers (Ball, 2008). One teacher, Jenny, linked the educational underachievement of working-class children to staff attitudes and not to their families:

> Some teachers still have a patronising and middle-class attitude towards both working class and ethnic minority children . . . we might as well go back to the Victorian era and send them to be house servants, because they're not academic. (Jenny, cited in Burn, 2001: 90)

Jenny's comments indicate some continuity with older 'deficit' discourses about working-class children. Other writers have suggested that there may be long-term societal prejudice against working-class children and their families (Skeggs, 1997; Byrne, 2005). For instance, Freire (1998: 62) argued that poor literacy rates could be directly linked to 'the existing contempt' that some teachers held for the children of the poor and their cultural practices. Writing of working-class families that have sometimes been categorized as difficult, disruptive and dysfunctional, Crozier and Reay (2005: x) claim that 'a new discourse is emerging around "hard to reach families" which . . . sets apart these families as different and implies a sense of inadequacy. Such parents are urged for example to take parenting lessons'.

Siobhan claimed that, in her experience, teachers sometimes held negative attitudes towards working-class parents.

> I think the attitude is that middle class parents support and help their kids at home and working class kids aren't supported and helped at home. (Siobhan, a white working-class teacher, cited in Burn, 2000c: 7).

Siobhan does not support the view that urban working-class parents are uninterested in their children's progress; she argues that, unlike middle-class families, they do not always have access to the necessary economic, educational and social capitals that would be necessary. She also commented that many of the mothers who were lone-carers, were simply exhausted by long hours working in poorly paid occupations, such as supermarket work, caring for senior citizens and cleaning, all work that reduced their capacity to give educational support to their children in the evenings (see also Reay, 1998).

Oliver, an Infant head teacher in an area of high poverty, identified and refuted the biased classed views that he had encountered.

> I've seen people come through the door and as soon as they start going, 'these sort of children. What do you expect from these sorts of children?' It's low expectation, it's that missionary zeal, which I really hate and deplore! I was one of these sorts of children. (Oliver, a mixed-race working-class head teacher, cited in Burn, 2005b: 194)

Oliver's observation that some teachers had what he described as a 'missionary zeal' towards poor urban children is reminiscent of the historical discourses of care and control that have already been described (Davin, 1996). Oliver, like Jenny, also believed that some teachers set out to 'save' poor working-class students from their 'undesirable' backgrounds while simultaneously holding low expectations of these children.

Carol, a Black working-class Early Years teacher, believed that the education system was biased against working-class children. She argued that the long-term expectation for working-class children (in schools and in society more generally) was that they would occupy routine and menial occupations (Burn, 2005a). hooks (2000: 45) describes how poor children and their families have often been portrayed in the media as 'parasites'. This depiction of the poor as lazy and as less capable of academic achievement echoes some of the historical discourses that have constructed urban families as needing to be 'controlled' and 'tamed' (Lee, 1987; Connolly, 1998; Byrne, 2005).

Ken (an Early Years teacher from a working-class background) suggested that because of the national testing regimes, the outcome was that poor working-class children were increasingly being publicly 'named and shamed':

> We're always comparing and comparing, you know, with the middle classes, they set the agenda, they set the rules. There are issues about children from other backgrounds . . . certain children get a better education. They have better access, better opportunities. (Ken, cited in Burn, 2005b: 168)

Working-class practitioners like Ken, Jenny and Carol identified financial disadvantage and structural bias as reasons that underlay working-class children's 'underachievement' in school. They believed that, from the start of their schooling, young children of the urban poor were discriminated against by some of the attitudes of some staff and by an inappropriate curriculum in the Early Years setting. Whatever the combination of factors that are implicated in the 'underachievement' of working-class urban children, the evidence that social background correlates with educational outcome is stark. Howard (2004) has researched how educational disadvantage is established from infancy onwards:

> By age two damage to educational development may have been done: 60 per cent of children from low-income groups who perform less well on child development tests at that age did not improve by age 10, and differences at 42 months strongly predict final educational qualifications. (Howard, 2004: 70)

Research carried out by Manchester University on white British children and their attainment, who qualify for free school meals, reports that a 'cycle of underachievement has been endemic in this group since mass education was introduced in Victorian times' (Crace, 2008: 1). However, the research did uncover 12 schools nationally that were able to boost the achievement of working-class children. They found that the teachers in these schools had 'a great sense of the community they serve. They understand their students' lives – often they come from the same sort of working-class background' (Crace, 2008: 2). These are also the characteristics of the Early Years teachers whose views have briefly been discussed in this part of the chapter; these teachers do not underestimate or stigmatize working-class children and their parents, because they come from similar backgrounds themselves.

Activity

To what extent do you think that television programmes such as the *Jeremy Kyle Show* or the *Jerry Springer Show* portray demeaning portraits of working-class families?

To what extent do you think that educational professionals hold low expectations of working-class families?

Current policy in Early Years (urban)

Now we want to consider some of the more recent policies that have been enacted by New Labour in the Early Years setting and consider the extent to which older discourses of 'care and control' have continued to shape this provision. Since coming to power in 1997, the New Labour governments have acknowledged the need for investment in Early Years provision, before and at the start of statutory schooling. They have recognized that investment in childhood makes economic and social sense for all those who want this provision and that one way to tackle social exclusion and disadvantage is through early support for 'disadvantaged' children and their families. However, in many ways, their policies of early intervention for children and families in areas of 'high deprivation' reflect earlier attempts that demeaned and demonized working-class families and their children rather than tackling wider structural and material injustices.

The New Labour focus on expanding and reforming Early Years education in 'deprived' areas is a very expensive attempt to tackle the long-standing educational underachievement of poor children within the education system (Hills et al., 2009). Sparkes and Glennerster (2002: 200), reviewing research from the London School of Economics, have concluded that 'intervention in a child's Early Years is among the most effective means of improving educational performance later'. This is a finding that New Labour has addressed in its policy-making directed to the Early Years setting. Ambitious targets have been set by New Labour to 'end child poverty within 20 years (2020)' (Flaherty et al., 2004: 144) and the start of the twenty-first century has been marked by an unprecedented expansion of pre-school provision. At the start of this chapter we argued that much Early Years policy has been shaped by a discourse of needing to 'save' the child (O'Connell Rust, 2003); this begs the question of whether rising social inequality is creating increased fears of the urban poor and is it this, rather than other more altruistic values that are shaping current policy?

In 1999, the government opened over 500 Sure Start programmes in areas of 'high deprivation', aimed at enhancing the life chances of poor children and their families. Sure Start is modelled on the Head Start programme that developed in urban America in the 1960s (Byrne, 2005). Children Centres have also been set up in areas of 'deprivation', to further support working-class families. A range of services are available, from advice on diet, to 'parenting' classes that encourage parents to read to their young children – although Gewirtz (2001) argues that these kinds of approaches are all about resocializing working-class parents. Multiple resources have been poured into these centres; for instance in 2007 every child was given a collection of picture books. In 2008, there were approaching 3,000 of these centres and the government plans to open an extra 500 Children Centres by 2010 (Ward, 2008). Bosely (2008: 12) found that 'the government's Sure Start programme appears to be succeeding in its aim of improving the chances of children born into deprived families'. But one question remains. Even if these provisions are excellent, and many of them are, to what degree do they overcome the influences of joblessness and poor housing? Unless policies are established simultaneously that address low wages, insecure work and the lack of good public housing, the long-term benefits may become eroded.

One assessment of Sure Start is that it is potentially a helpful and highly supportive initiative for parents and young children (Toynbee and Walker, 2008). However, the Parliamentary Health Committee (2008) reported that in certain urban areas there were 'concerns that Sure Start programmes were being "colonized" by the middle classes, who enjoyed the cheap, high quality childcare they offer and that extending provision universally would further dilute their focus on those who need them the most'. Another point of concern relates to the content and approach of some of these interventions. The state's eye is clearly focused on the 'correct' development for children of the urban poor for, as Byrne (2005: 159) points out, 'only the children of the poor are meant to be in Sure Start'. It is the children of the poor and their parents who require such state intervention. Unlike other more radical approaches where families are respected as repositories of knowledge to be tapped into, many of the UK initiatives start from a 'professional' approach in 'supporting' and augmenting the role of the family that speaks of partnership, but does not always involve them in active participation.

The introduction of a curriculum from birth is another major strategy ostensibly aimed at delivering equality and ensuring that 'Every Child Matters'. The 2008 legislation combines the Standards for care, health and safety with specific educational targets for all settings (including childminders) from birth to five years of age. The new Early Years Curriculum and the testing of the very youngest children (0–5 years) may well be one of the most comprehensive curriculum interventions since the beginning of state schooling in the 1870s. All Early Years settings will be inspected by Ofsted to ensure compliance with this curriculum. A profile is required to be drawn up (by the providers) of individual children's scores on set targets and a final assessment (Profile Scales) will be produced prior to the child entering Infant School at the age of five. Children who are underachieving in literacy, numeracy and personal social education will be identified and subject to further interventions (DCSF, 2008).

In 2007, Profile results were published, based on the previous Foundation Stage Curriculum for 3- to 5-year-olds. These results showed significant differences in achievement, with Early Years providers in predominately poor working-class areas reporting the lowest scores. Similarly, inspection of childminders showed how those in 'poorer areas are failing to provide a good service' (Garner, 2008: 8). For example, in Woking, an affluent area of Surrey, 81 per cent of childminding was good or better; however, in Hackney, an area of high disadvantage in London, only 29 per cent of childminders were rated as 'good' (Garner, 2008). The children's director of Ofsted, Michael Hart is 'concerned that children in more deprived areas do not, on the whole, have access to as much good provision as others. This cannot help overcome disadvantage' (cited in Garner, 2008: 8). Thus, not unexpectedly, social class is strongly implicated in the quality of provision and practice in this sector.

One more point of concern relates to the enormous amount of data that is being collected about the educational progress of young working-class children. Any wider debate into the ethics behind this state monitoring of very young children who live in 'disadvantaged' families is still to take place. In their earlier study of child-rearing practices, Walkerdine and Lucey (1989: 181) warned that

> The whole discourse of parental involvement assumes that teachers must teach parents (almost always mothers) how to prepare and help their children in the right ways. The target is, almost always, black and white working-class parents. There is no sense of listening to and learning from the parents – for they are already defined as wrong and reactionary.

Critical questions need to be addressed to the approaches being currently taken in the Early Years setting that may still reflect this damaging and demonizing approach towards the urban child and their family.

Policy alternatives

Things do not have to be this way. There are alternatives. For example, the Reggio Emilia approach to the education of young children is based on completely different assumptions about children, parents and carers, pedagogy and curriculum. This approach, based on interactions between children, parents and teachers, was started by Loris Malaguzzi just after the Second World War in southern Italy. It has been implemented in many national settings and is internationally celebrated (Cadwell, 2002). At the heart of this way of working is a belief that children are competent learners and that parents are the 'first teachers'. There is no expressed curriculum. Rather, Reggio Emilia approaches emphasize the need to allow children to control their learning through exploring their environments, following their own curiosity, through problem-solving and through trusting the children to make the right decisions. Children and teachers work in the same groups for a period of up to three years and the teacher is a co-learner in a joint enterprise with the children and the other adults who learn with the child. Parents and carers, and the local community are involved in decisions about learning. There are school committees, 'La Consulta', that inform policy-making at a local level.

The Reggio Emilia approach mirrors a social-constructivist approach towards supporting and extending learning. The curriculum is constructed out of a range of different starter points; for example, a child's enquiry, a parent's question, a teacher's concern. It is also constructed out of detailed observations and reflections on the spontaneous play of the children. Teachers work alongside the children to follow their interests and responses rather than through imposing a predetermined formulaic curriculum that may have little resonance with, or respect for, the experiences and concerns of the children and their families. The Reggio approach has an emancipatory project, one that would sit well in the urban setting (Lewin-Benham, 2005). However, policy and pedagogical attempts that split off education work from the structural and material context run the risk of missing the mark.

Activity

Go to the City Neighbours Charter School website and see what you can find out about the Reggio Emilia approach to Early Years education.
   http://www.cityneighbors.org/reggioemilia.html
   What aspects of this approach could provide a more respectful and empowering curriculum in the urban Early Years setting?

Conclusion

Ball and Vincent (2005: 206) argue that New Labour's 'emphasis on access, on bringing childcare to those families who did not have such options, is highly laudable'. However, as we have already pointed out, Early Years policy is a compression of many interwoven strands of policy – a policy ensemble of older and newer discourses. Thus, as we have argued in this chapter, the current expansion of urban Early Years education is tied into continuities in state concerns for the children of the poor. If we compare what is being attempted now with earlier responses there are some similar policy drives, such as a fear of and the need to 'civilize' the urban working-class child. Without a more radical and contextualized approach, that starts from a complex spatial analysis and that works in a reciprocal way with families and children, there will be some small improvements, but no real change in the status quo. There is a fundamental contradiction. If we know that some groups of children tend to do less well than others, then shouldn't we do something to address this inequality? However, it is *what* we do and *how* we do it that is the critical issue. In the Early Years setting, more radical approaches that start by respecting what families bring with them and extending decision-making responsibility to parents and carers, rather than being driven by the concerns of professionals, seem a long way off. In neo-liberal times, where education is tightly conformed to labour market requirements rather than fulfilment or empowerment, one of the saddest outcomes is that this 'economistic' approach has now been inserted into the schooling of the very youngest children. In this flurry of reform activity, Early Years urban education may still be at risk of being constructed as a 'rescue' operation for the working-class child carried out by substitute 'mothers' and assessed by a paternalistic state.

Further reading

Charlesworth, V. (2009) *Critical Skills in the Early Years*. London: Network Continuum Education.

Pratt-Adams, S. and Maguire, M. (2009) 'Urban primary school headship in England: an emotional perspective', *Critical Studies in Education*, 50, (2) June 2009: 115–127.

Smidt, S. (2009) (2nd edn) *Key Issues in Early Years Education: A Guide for Students and Practitioners*. London: Routledge.

Thornton, L. and Brunton, P. (2009) *Understanding The Reggio Approach: Early Years Education In Practice*. London: David Fulton.

Useful websites

Early Years Foundation Stage Curriculum at: http://www.teachernet.gov.uk/teachingandlearning/EYFS/British Association for Early Childhood Education at http://www.early-education.org.uk/

Urban Education and New and Emergent Learning Technologies

9

Chapter Outline

Introduction

This chapter explores the place of new and emergent technologies, the internet and E-learning in relation to urban education. It reviews plans for the schooling of the future and the prospect of virtual school communities and reflects on the notion that teaching and learning may no longer be based on spatial or geographical location but will increasingly take place virtually. The issue of educational inequalities is also discussed in terms of the surfacing of digital inclusion and exclusion alongside other forms of inequity in the twenty-first century. The chapter concludes by critically considering the extent to which new and emergent learning technologies, including mobile learning, have the potential to transform education in urban contexts.

New and emergent technologies and E-learning

Information and communication technology (ICT) has been in schools since the 1980s and it has been claimed (DfES, 2005; Puttnam, 2008) that its impact on school populations can transform learning, particularly for those students who have previously been excluded from the learning process. There are examples of E-learning transforming individual urban schools, through offering a more flexible curriculum and improved access to resources (Purnell, 2005), although it has been argued that significant stakeholders, such as students and teachers have been marginalized and silenced from policy formation (Sinfield et al., 2010).

It is now well understood that E-learning is not simply about the implementation and use of technical tools but particularly with the use of the internet, it is concerned with the nature and use of knowledge and information. Indeed, governments speak of the inescapability of technological change (Pearson, 2004). Proponents of the merits of E-learning and particularly online activity see it as assisting in moving towards a more democratic, inclusive society (e-Learning Foundation, 2006). However, while it may be the case that we are entering *a new age* through the use of an increasingly important technology, others have claimed that its impact in transforming lives might be overstated (Cuban, 2001; Loader and Keeble, 2005).

Education is a key social institution as it creates, reflects and responds to the prevailing needs of society. On the one hand, it is alleged that much human employment activity is now based around practices that require an educated, professional, technologically adept workforce (DfES, 2005). On the other hand, there is a danger of education not meeting the needs of individuals and communities; but *warehousing* and producing people to meet national targets that suit the needs of industry for a graduate labour force that is competitive and flexible, but for many manifests itself into low pay and insecure employment.

People growing up in the information society in the twenty-first century will, it is argued, require new and different forms of pedagogy in schools in order to be ICT literate, to be able to use ICT to advance their learning and participate in the economy. Of course this will require a high level of educational or technological resourcing to support an ICT-rich curriculum in urban schools, without which there will be inequality of access between those who get to control knowledge and information and those who do not.

The notion of a learning society has been common parlance for some time (Schon, 1973; Hutchins, 1970). The learning city, region or community, as many areas now claim to be, have embraced this development, supporting among other attributes lifelong learning initiatives, where learning in the form of knowledge and information is available for anyone, any time, any place (Husen, 1974; Longworth, 2006). Much of this learning focuses on the importance of how new learning technologies can make a difference by stimulating teaching and learning, particularly in low-income, urban areas. Learning is seen to be at the heart of social and cultural change. Thus, there is a need to ensure that the technological education that is delivered in urban locales is of the highest quality to prepare young people for life in a technological world.

Changing schooling

The internet has begun to offer alternatives to a more traditional understanding of school. Examples of this include City Learning Centres in England as part of the Excellence in Cities (EiC) programme providing E-learning opportunities in disadvantaged areas and the Smart Cities initiative in New York where the Board of Education plans to improve education using E-learning both in-school and out. According to a Becta report (2007) in the UK, the effective use of E-learning has the potential to improve schools in terms of achievement and progress. The report claimed that Primary School leaders who invested strategically in E-learning, both in terms of resources and human expertise and training raised overall results and standards. Furthermore, E-learning was also seen to have an indirect influence in terms of raised self-esteem, more engagement, better behaviour and attendance, particularly with more disadvantaged students (Hollingworth et al., 2008). As will be discussed below, issues remain around funding technologies and possibilities of transforming traditional pedagogies.

E-learning can lower the barriers that were erected in older models of learning (Hollingworth et al., 2008). The school buildings of the past can be replaced by more flexible learning communities, not based on geographical location, distance or time. However, it has also been argued that internet use might have little impact on inequalities in the education system (Lee, 2008). Some aspects of education will still require face-to-face contact and therefore there will continue to be some need for central sites to provide such services. Many of today's learners are able to blend their learning between E-learning and more traditional approaches in ways that make learning uniquely advantageous to their learning needs (JISC, 2007). A *blended* approach to learning that integrates both physical and virtual worlds can, for instance, offer supportive group learning. So students are able to adapt and apply learning to their own needs. Back in 1995, Tiffin and Rajasingham stated:

> People accept limitations on what they learn because of where they live. The virtual class opens the possibility that any learner, no matter where they are, could be put in touch with any teacher, in any area of knowledge, that addresses any problem domain. (1995: 162)

A vision of the school of the future is one where learning is continuous and innovative, as it will be necessary to adapt to different and ever-changing learning situations, allowing communities to become empowered by being connected around the world. ICT is a significant element in supporting such a vision when applied to learning, as there are many different ways that learning can occur: 'Mak(ing) it possible for more individuals than ever to access knowledge and to learn in new and different ways' (Kerrey and Isakson, 2000: foreword).

Inclusion and exclusion

Many schools in technologically rich societies are now connected to the internet, with UK figures stating that around 90 per cent of 12- to 24-year-olds are using the internet (Social Trends, 2006; Lenhart et al., 2007). New technologies can transform the learning experience of learners, offer new opportunities and have the potential to address issues of social exclusion that can be found within education (DfES, 2005; Hollingworth et al., 2008). E-learning can also offer a range of learning strategies and can be inspiring for some learners because it is more visual, interactive, flexible and student controlled.

However, not everybody is well served. Although E-learning is being posited as a panacea to overcome social inequalities, it has the potential to further render silent the already marginalized. Therefore this becomes a political as well as a pedagogic issue. Research is now indicating that those people who are socially excluded in terms of employment, income, health and education, are likely to be excluded from the information society. Indeed, digital exclusion can combine with other forms of deprivation to increase and intensify inequality and exclusion (Castells, 2002). Furthermore, it has been argued that the emergence of the information society has created new forms of inequality (Flecha, 1999). Indeed, Castells has claimed: 'The Information Age does not have to be the age of stepped-up inequality, polarisation and social exclusion. But for the moment it is' (2002: 129).

According to an analysis of digital exclusion by the UK Department for Communities and Local Government, 'technology and social disadvantages are inextricably linked' (Helsper, 2008: 15). Digital exclusion has been viewed by the UK government as being one of the most damaging forms of social exclusion as both cause and symptom of wider exclusion in society as a result of socio-economic status and deprivation (Castells, 2002; Helsper, 2008). Moreover, Pearson claims:

> On the one hand, if technologies are shaped by social conditions, then they will inevitably reflect the values and norms of the particular society in which they are created. On the other hand, if we believe technology determines the way society develops, then we might feel very helpless and fatalistic. (Pearson, 2004: 1.3)

There is a correlation between socio-economic background and access to the internet and the services that it has to offer. While technology can have a role to play in addressing inequalities, there are concerns that urban school populations and school systems in 'low-income' neighbourhoods are lagging behind in the technological world as they have been doing in the industrial world (Tettegah, 2005). As was pointed out by Becta's IMPACT 2 study in 2006, the level of access in the UK is clearly related to socio-economic status. Mossberger et al. (2003: 136) note: 'Those without skills have little need to use computers, and those without frequent availability have little chance to develop the skills.' For instance, the gap between E-learning availability can be seen between private and public educational settings. Jia Qi reports that in urban Taiwan, fee-paying schools are enthusiastic to purchase the latest technologies as a key marketing tool to attract potential students and they seek to take advantage of E-learning opportunities. Yet, state organizations and underprivileged groups are neglected and benefit little from E-learning programmes – 'The most in need failed to benefit the most from the E-learning trend' (Jia Qi, 2005: 45).

It has been claimed that accessibility to learning technologies promises to reduce social exclusion for disadvantaged communities, enabling all people to take part in social and community life as well as enhancing educational opportunities (Carr-Chellman, 2005). In order to avoid such social divisions, school, according to Hess and Leal (1999: 370) can play an important role in bridging the widening gap between the 'informational "haves" and the "have nots"'. Research by these authors exploring the integration of information technologies into urban classrooms in the US found that demographic and institutional variables had a significant effect on computer use in classrooms. However, what was most surprising was that high-income districts did not provide more computer training in school. It was surmised that this may have been because children from high-income households already received more computer exposure at home or in other places, such as libraries.

Disengagement with digital resources is a complex issue in society. For children and young people the issue is not only about access and non-access, but is also related to effective use of the technology for educational purposes and this impacts many schools in low-income neighbourhoods (McAdoo, 2000). For Livingstone et al. (2005: 4) 'The idea of a divide (of haves and have nots) is less useful than the idea of a continuum from hesitant, narrow or unskilled use to diverse, confident and skilled use of the Internet'. So the impact of low levels of knowledge of the users can also hinder effective use.

Reduced access to the internet can limit life chances and learning opportunities for socially and economically disadvantaged groups – 'the bandwidth-disadvantaged' (Mitchell, 1995: 17) who may also be considerably disadvantaged in other ways in society (Lee, 2008). Lack of access to the internet and what it offers can increase exclusion and reduce peoples' social and cultural capital as well as economic opportunities that result from this. While the number of people in the UK lacking basic ICT skills has reduced according to the Digital Britain Final Report (DCMS, 2009), a significant proportion continue to be excluded.

There also remains a chasm in access between those in full-time employment in valuable, intellectual work and those who are in 'non-valuable' work, fractional work or are unemployed and these people may fall further behind in the digital economy. The Digital Britain Final Report (DCMS, 2009) stated that '22 million employees use technology daily in the workforce'. However, some less advantaged students may only be prepared for the lower rungs of the technological industries while others will have the right skills and be in the right place to participate more centrally in the new technologies economy (Hess and Leal, 1999).

In this regard then access to ICT and E-learning becomes a new form of cultural capital (FitzPatrick and Conway, 2005). McAdoo sees this process as following the example of the Industrial Revolution: 'Remaking class divisions in the old "factory model" of schooling, instead of envisioning a technological future that is enriching and democratic across class lines' (2000: 145). Indeed, Sinfield et al. (2010) claim that E-learning policy is a fight by the state to take control back from the potential democracy of the internet.

Research among 9- to 19-year-olds in the UK has found that middle-class children have more online experience, take up more of the available online opportunities and benefit from higher quality access (Livingstone et al., 2005). In another study of 1024 young people aged 14 to 23 years, selected through random sampling in Germany, it was found that there were inequalities in terms of internet use. Social inequalities and different educational backgrounds influenced internet use, and in so doing, access to education opportunities (Iske et al., 2008). However, technological inclusion is not necessarily the answer to reducing inequalities and exclusion in society as

> The impact of the Internet is indeed much more temporary and limited, and is unable to deal with the wider range of disadvantages suffered by young people from poorer backgrounds which need to be addressed alongside digital in/exclusion. (Lee, 2008: 151)

While it can be argued that there are other factors in society that might be more significant in determining life chances and social mobility, lack of access to digital resources reinforces and amplifies inequality and may create new forms of inequality.

Home access

In terms of having the internet at home, those in society with the greatest need frequently have the least access to the resources. Higher income households are more likely to have internet access at home than lower income households with 87 per cent to 18 per cent between the highest and lowest quintiles in the UK (Social Trends, 2006). Advanced quality home access allows users to participate in more advanced digital activities (Helsper, 2008). Furthermore, more and more schools put resources into Managed Learning Environments, which means that children living in homes that have the internet will have more opportunity to develop their learning through greater access to online resources. This is supported by a study of young people's internet use among different schools in Brighton, England, where

> Out-of-class availability was markedly better in the independent schools which provided open access IT rooms. Students at the comprehensive school in contrast often had few opportunities outside their weekly IT lessons to access the Internet, and these students also had much lower levels of home access. (Lee, 2008: 146)

An initiative aimed at addressing students' reduced access to home computers and instruction has taken place at Broadgreen High School, located in a low-income area of Liverpool. It set up a scheme to raise funds with parents to buy laptops that could be leased out. Evidence suggests the initiative has improved both homework and school attendance (Strategy Unit, 2005). However, access to the technology or equipment is not necessarily sufficient. There are many families on low incomes that do not, or cannot get network connection as not all people have the income to pay for internet access. So while E-learning can break down certain barriers, such as space and time, other barriers such as financial ones remain. Thus, one of the objectives of the UK's Children, Schools and Families Implementation Plan (2009–2012) for *Harnessing Technology for Next Generation Learning* aims to:

> Ensure(ing) that home access entitlement is delivered to all learners, and especially those who are hard to reach and those at risk of digital exclusion, and that technology adds value to family and extended learning, and learners use technology confidently and responsibly to support their learning and access to information. (Becta, 2009a: 4)

Some families may be less able to provide support than others (Livingstone et al., 2005). Therefore, it is important to provide home support as research has found that parents of middle-class children have more expertise in terms of internet literacy. One recent UK initiative is the 'Home Access Programme' that involves the computer company RM providing a range of computers, software, internet access and support initially to low-income families in urban Oldham (as well as in the largely rural county of Suffolk). It is intended to develop this pilot into a national initiative, aimed at providing equal learning opportunities to the 35 per cent of families that currently have no access to the internet at home to provide both social and educational benefits (Becta, 2008a; Becta, 2009b). Another example is the One Laptop per Child initiative making $100 laptops available to economically developing nations (OLPC, 2008).

Since 2004, the e-learning Foundation has been working in the UK to achieve equality of access to computers and the internet in schools and in homes. The aim is to support learning through financial assistance from their Digital Divide Fund and campaigns to develop effective home–school ICT use. Urban regions receiving grants in 2006 included Bolton, Wolverhampton and Portsmouth as well as major UK cities. Berger Primary School in the London borough of Hackney was one recipient of a grant from the e-learning

Foundation for a project in 2005–6 to provide home computers for families, thereby extending learning between home and school. Open access to school and college facilities and City Learning Centres during evenings and weekends, supported by the e-learning Foundation, has also been successful (DfES, 2005).

One relatively successful project was Lambeth Link-Up which aimed at bridging the digital divide by increasing internet access for residents on two estates in this inner London borough (SustainIT, 2006). Initiatives included installing an ICT suite in a community centre, offering basic training and free computer and internet use. Free or cheap home-based internet access was also provided for those who did not use the centre. However, follow-up funding for the project has been hard to obtain and has hampered the sustainability of the project. As is the case here, disadvantaged local authorities may not have sufficient resources to match governmental funding in comparison to more advantaged communities. Community-based technology centres that are based in low-income neighbourhoods have also been seen as valuable by the US Department of Education, who has provided funding for these to be set up in community settings (Chen, 2000).

Computers are powerful tools, but tools themselves are not that important; rather it is what we do with them that is vital (Tiffin and Rajasingham, 1995). ICT has the potential to intervene in human tasks and social issues, but also to reinforce or alleviate social division. Therefore ethical considerations become paramount.

Activity

In an unequal society and within the current education system, is there any way that those marginalized within society can engage with, *bridge* and overcome the digital divide themselves?

Explore the website for young people called Britkid that addresses the issue of 'race' and racism in schools (www.Britkid.org). Critically consider issues that could be inferred from an initiative like this about morally improving and *civilizing* urban children.

Transforming education?

E-learning, in theory, allows learners alternatives to traditional learning through the flexibility of studying at a pace and time that suits their personal, independent needs; for instance, people who are working and studying, those who cannot afford travel costs and those that are sick or house-bound. E-learning enables schooling to go beyond the confines of the school building such as through the utilization of information retrieval systems. Although it must always be noted that there is the potential here that this revolution can exacerbate and make visible already existing inequalities that enriches the already advantaged and can further isolate the poor.

One example within the urban context of utilizing the potential of E-learning comes from the London Borough of Haringey, where many of the students speak English as an additional language. Primary school pupils participated in a literacy project, accessing interactive games linked to the National Literacy Strategy. The DfES (2005: 42) reported that 83 per cent of students enrolled on the programme regularly used the games, with teachers praising 'the use of higher order questions to encourage children to think about abstract concepts'. In this instance we find E-learning responding to and adapting a national strategy to meet local urban needs. This is the type of initiative that has the potential to enhance and make credible the claims of E-learning.

It has been suggested that online study can also be more efficient and economical than face-to-face learning, with its potential for reducing bureaucracy and administration (Carr-Chellman, 2005). However, others claim that in the higher education context, it puts pressure on already overstretched academics, leaving even less time to reflect on critical pedagogy, while increasing bureaucracy and administrative costs (Sinfield et al., 2010). Furthermore, curriculum content and teaching materials can be stored on a secure internet management system that is accessible any time or place. This has the potential to truly liberate the student to take control of their learning. However, there is a shadow side to these central (intranet) systems that allows for increased policing and monitoring of the *transgressive* student. So instead of becoming a flexible resource for students, it can be used in a reductionist fashion that becomes more prescriptive.

This technology has the potential to extend learning to individuals and whole communities, who for geographical, political, cultural or social reasons are neglected or suppressed, by offering a creative, dynamic space that can be truly democratizing. Yet independence gained from E-learning can also have a negative impact in terms of disconnectedness (James, 1998; Palmer, 2007). Therefore, there is a tension here that has yet to be resolved.

E-learning in urban contexts

The ICT Excellence Awards is a scheme for schools which aims to identify and reward whole school technological excellence and achievement. Schools are encouraged to use a self-review framework to evaluate how they are managing their use of ICT and E-learning. The best whole school national winner for Secondary Schools in 2008 was Djanogly City Academy in Nottingham. The school is situated in an inner-city area, with many children on free school meals, who speak English as an additional language and who have reading scores below the national average. The award was for the development of its Learning Gateway and integrated management information system. The school also uses wireless projectors and tablet computers in classroom teaching (Becta, 2008b).

Arguably, E-learning gives students and teachers an edge, when teachers take responsibility and reflect on their use of technologies in schools and how these resources can be used to extend learning. Virtual school trips have the potential to provide support for learning experiences such as field work activities, whereby students are able to move around virtual space to explore the real thing, but from a distance. This could include a virtual path through a website or using a map with 'hotspots' that allows the students to experience a subject in more detail so as to construct their own knowledge of that subject. Caution needs to be taken though in merely producing binary oppositions between 'real' and virtual life, for as Nunes points out: 'Perhaps this distinction is not so cut-and-dried. Certainly the space we are calling cyberspace neither begins nor ends at the computer screen' (2006: 11).

Virtual world applications such as Second Life are particularly useful as they offer collaborative and interactive uses in three-dimensional environments for multidisciplinary educational and training purposes, as well as leisure-based uses (de Freitas, 2008). They present possibilities for experiential modes of teaching and learning using simulations and immersive role play and scenarios to simulate real life. They allow the user to explore situations and carry out research in artificially created environments. An example of this was a case study that examined what happened when a historical simulation game *Civilization III* was introduced to a class in an urban high school in a north-eastern city in the US (Squire and Barab, 2004). The class was being required to repeat the year as they had failed ninth grade and lacked engagement in their learning. In terms of educational implications, the students developed familiarity with gaming concepts, problem-solving skills and deeper understanding of several academic subjects including advanced forms of literacy as well as history, a subject often rejected by marginalized students as it can be presented as an un-contentious, de-contextualized truth (Loewen, 1995). *Civilization III*, in contrast, enabled players 'to examine how their civilization grows culturally, geographically, scientifically, and politically over time' (Squire and Barab, 2004: 2). This then allowed them to be aware of their power and agency.

This type of application also extends distance, online and flexible delivery and communication between learners, beyond more established forms of ICTs such as email and chatrooms. These forms of learning will soon become commonplace, as many young people are already familiar with virtual worlds found in computer-based modelled world simulations and games as well as text-based chatrooms. The scope of social interactions and exchanges, using for instance social networking applications, is also broad in terms of bringing groups and communities together to support democratic development; for instance it is valuable for students with disabilities and those with difficulties with social communication (Shepherd, 2007; de Freitas, 2008). The Global Kids project (www.globalkids.org) based in New York City is one example that uses (Teen) Second Life activities and games to raise young people's awareness of human rights, the environment and citizenship. The project consists of a series of interrelated programs designed to encourage and support teenagers in thinking critically about the role of digital media in their lives, promote constructive use of new media forms and document their experiences. Within the program, participants use contests, online dialogues, a virtual world, podcasts, blogs and so forth to gather valuable feedback and views from other young people about their relationship with emerging media; therefore they have greater power and choice in constructing their own identities.

In terms of pedagogy, some theorists (Smith et al., 2006; Selwyn, 1999) question how much impact the use of computerized technologies has in relation to traditional forms, although others see new technologies as causing a shift in terms of social impact by integrating computers and society more closely (Turkle, 1997). As early as 1997, Oppenheimer was writing about what he termed the 'computer delusion' regarding the perceived benefits of the increased use of computers in schools and other settings.

While the rhetoric is that E-learning can help the neediest in society to gain access to educational opportunities, Carr-Chellman maintains that such a technological system 'cannot truly serve our most needy' (2005: 155) and that digital rhetoric will not of itself improve an individual's social situation. There will be limited benefits for those operating at the margins of society and digital exclusion can contribute to deepen social exclusion rather than improve it (Helsper, 2008). It should be recognized then that technological innovations need to be sensitive and responsive to the needs of those constituents, including those in urban settings, who are economically, socially and perhaps now digitally disadvantaged.

Activity

How could the examples of critical pedagogy derived from Freire and hooks (see Chapter 7) be harnessed within technology-based teaching and learning in urban contexts?

Mobile urban learning

A shortcoming of E-learning has been that in the past the learning experiences have frequently been limited to the institutional setting, whereas mobile learning (or M-learning), using mobile phone technologies and ever more pervasive internet capability opens up new learning opportunities for more people. Mobile learning can bridge the gap between formal and informal learning (Cook et al., 2008). A user-centred perspective recognizes that it is the learner who is on the move and active; the device, whether personal digital assistant (PDA), smartphone or portable personal computer (PC) is secondary. Portable technologies are embedded in learning contexts to support tasks and activities, allowing students to utilize appropriate materials whether they are off-site, on campus or independent of specific locales. They can also offer students ways of continually generating new knowledge and extending this to others in a community of learners (Cook et al., 2008).

One example of the interplay between mobile learning technologies and the urban context was a pedagogical initiative developed by one of the authors of this book. The setting for the initiative was a working-class neighbourhood in North London, an area steeped in diverse social and cultural traditions.

The initiative was intended to enrich university students' knowledge and understanding of this urban context by using mobile learning technologies to immerse them in the setting. Moreover, it supported the generation of new knowledge by the intersection of their connectivity to each other, the context and expert systems, demonstrating and extending a reflexive self within a community of practice (Giddens, 1996; Lave and Wenger, 1998).

The use of a historical perspective demonstrated continuation, change and causation enabling a better understanding of both contemporary and possible future urban education contexts. The project presented digital materials such as historical maps, old photographs of students, oral histories and interactive quick-time video shoots of the key buildings as mobile learning objects for users to use on high-end mobile phones and PCs. Using GPS (Global Positioning System) technology to pinpoint their location, enabled users, when combined with 'real' presence, to examine past and present representations of urban settings and relate these to a contemporary study of urban education.

The initiative had several objectives: first, to explore how schools are signifiers of both urban change and continuity in education policy and practice in one inner-city locale; second, to explore urbanism and urbanization by examining the flows of diverse peoples within urban space and infrastructures (Castells, 1996). Third, the initiative provided evidence of how the organization and (re)structuring of urban space, in particular related to religious practices work(ed) alongside educational discourses and policies to support participation in civic urban life and educate generations of working-class children. Finally, the aim was to examine the community from the past, in order to engage with, understand and inform the present, as urban space and society becomes made and remade.

The project used a complex interplay between mobile learning technologies, iconic physical infrastructures and educational discourses to visualize urban education through various collective images and representations in order to create a digital urban 'technoscape' (Appadurai, 1996; Sheller and Urry, 2006). Using a combination of social and cultural scripts or scenarios displayed on mobile phones in real time as they walked and inhabited the urban space, the intention was for the student to *move through* the re-constructed landscape and thus 'perform that landscape' (Sheller and Urry, 2006: 9). Within this virtual and real environment students had the opportunity to examine the habitus of the past, while generating new practices and knowledges (Bourdieu, 1977).

Activity

Critically evaluate and discuss the impact of mobile learning for both the educator and the student in the urban context.

Conclusion

Earlier chapters have discussed the shift in the nineteenth century from a largely agricultural economy to a manufacturing one, as a result of the industrial revolution. At the beginning of the twenty-first century, ICTs are defining modern society and have created enormous social changes, for instance in terms of work, lifestyle and communication.

E-learning has the capability to transform lives. Arguably, there are great benefits in the ways that information and knowledge have been made accessible, particularly for those who are isolated and disadvantaged, by supporting those who previously had poor experiences of education. However, it has been noted in this chapter that E-learning has the potential to perpetuate inequality. It has been shown that technology, when it is used in a democratizing, transparent and inclusive manner can be part of the solution rather than part of the problem.

Further reading

Becta (2009a) *Harnessing Technology for Next Generation Learning Children, Schools and Families Implementation Plan 2009–2012.* Coventry: Becta.

Carr-Chellman, A. (2005) (ed.) *Global Perspectives on E-learning: Rhetoric and Reality.* London: Sage.

Hollingworth, S., Allen, K., Hutchings, M., Kuyok, K. and Williams, K. (2008) *Technology and School Improvement: Reducing Social Inequity with Technology?* http://partners.becta.org.uk/upload-dir/downloads/page_documents/research/school_improvement_final_report.pdf. 'Technology, Pedagogy and Education', *Journal of the Association of Information Technology in Teacher Education* (*ITTE*), published by Routledge, Taylor and Francis Group.

Useful websites

http://www.becta.org.uk/
Becta (British Educational Communications and Technology Agency)

http://www.e-learningfoundation.com/
e-Learning Foundation
http://www.lse.ac.uk/collections/children-go-online
UK Children Go Online Project Website

Part 4
Changing Urban Education

In this last part, we draw together all the threads of this book. In the introduction, we talked of the need for critical hope, something to which we return in this final chapter. What we hope to have demonstrated in this book is that 'more of the same' will simply not do. What is needed is a critical urban pedagogy that is inclusive, organic, creative and emancipatory.

Justice, Hope and Vision

Introduction

In this last chapter, we want to pull together three of the substantive issues that have permeated the discussions and debates within this book. First, we want to consider change and continuity in the schooling of the urban working classes over time, for critical urban sociology has always insisted on the need for a historical dimension in understanding the city (Grace, 1984). Second, we want to pose some questions about changing urban education, our central task. As we have argued, there is an urgent need to change and extend how we understand the city and the urban experience. There is also an equally urgent need to change what we do in urban schools. Finally, we want to continue the argument and the struggle for justice, hope and vision for working-class children and their schools, wherever they are located.

Continuity over time

One of the themes of this book is that when we explore education policy designed for urban settings or when we look at the challenges that impact the urban school, there seem to be strong continuities with the past. We have argued that the education that was provided for working-class children in the nineteenth century and into the first half of the twentieth century was never intended to be emancipatory; initially it was intended to provide young urban dwellers with the sorts of rudimentary skills and attitudes that would fit them up for working-class jobs. The education that was on offer was not designed to help young people to become empowered or reflexive; rather, the regimes and practices of schooling were designed to reproduce a 'gentled', docile and obedient work force (Johnson, 1976).

Activity

What continuities can you identify between current policies and practices and the schools of the past?

What changes would you like to see in (a) the curriculum and (b) the way that urban classrooms are organized?

In this book we have also highlighted the ways in which the state, driven by the fears and anxieties of the middle classes about the threats posed to and the social order by the 'unruly' working classes, sought to intervene in the parenting and, specifically, the 'mothering' of the very young working-class child, in order to 'fix' the problem. The church provided schooling that concentrated on saving the soul rather than challenging oppressions. Always the problem was seen as a 'deficit' or 'lack' that, once addressed, would result in the production of a 'gentled' and submissive member of the working class. This is a policy approach that has had a long reach down the years.

However, this view of the early provision of state education might be regarded as somewhat selective and perhaps simplistic, for in reality, provisions are always more complex and contested. Over the years, many individual schools and teachers have struggled to provide a decent and extended education for working-class children (Wrigley, 2006). For example, Annie and

Tom Higdon set up the famous Burston Strike School in order to ensure that working-class (rural) children were able to attend school rather than do casual harvesting work in the fields of their parents' employers, the local landowners (Edwards, 1974). This was the longest strike in the history of the UK (1914–39). In the second half of the twentieth century, the provision of free Secondary Education for all children marked another key milestone in the history of provision for working-class children. However, it is hard to escape from the conclusion that, in the main, education remains stratified and UK society is still divided and unequal (Wilkinson and Pickett, 2009). Change, that is real change, is hard to achieve and slow to come.

Education policy-making by the state has rarely been a radical venture. Frequently, ideas that have been tried in the past are reworked and re-circulated into the contemporary setting. For example, the divided and segregated schooling of the late nineteenth and early twentieth centuries is still reflected in the provision of the Academy schools, the remaining grammar schools and the faith schools that together make up a significant part of the contemporary state-maintained sector. There is also the almost 'untouchable' English public school system that continues to exert enormous influence and still facilitates disproportionate access to social advantage in the cultural and material world of the twenty-first century (Tomlinson, 2008). There is still evidence of Freire's (1970) 'banking' approach in the content-driven National Curriculum and its onerous assessment mechanisms. Even in the recent New Labour periods of government, where education has ostensibly been prioritized (Hills et al., 2009), while there have been undeniable reforms, there are still many continuities with the past. For example, as Ball (2008: 197) says, 'no government, Conservative or Labour, has been willing to take seriously the idea of a common system of education'.

Writing of the changes brought about by the Elementary School Act in 1870, Simon (1965: 363) stated that these developments were 'not merely a story of philanthropy and growing enlightenment, resulting in a continuous upward curve of development but rather a history of breakthroughs and retreats . . . nothing is gained (or retained) without persistent and determined pressure'. The same could be said of more recent educational reforms. However, some changes in access to education have occurred, such as the extension of the compulsory phase of schooling, the inclusion of children designated as having 'special needs', the massification of higher education and the undoubted success of female students. These changes have all reached the urban school and the urban world. But Ball (2008: 194) suggests that there are still questions about 'the extent of "real" change in "real" schools'. He points to the enduring continuities with the past, notably in terms of 'the social differentiations that were part of the basic building blocks of state education in the nineteenth century, especially those involving social class' (Ball, 2008: 195).

Barber (2009: 19) has claimed that 'There are academics who use sophisticated statistical techniques to support the view that social background remorselessly determines outcomes, regardless of what education systems do'. The difficulty is that so much of the available evidence does suggest that this connection between social class and educational outcome persists (ONS, 2005; Taylor, 2006). As Reay (2006: 304) notes: 'the attainment gap between the classes is just as great as it was 20, 50 years ago and mirrors the growing material gap between the rich and the poor in UK society'.

Activity

What three things would you do to seriously improve urban schools?

Changing urban education

Another key theme of this book is woven into its title which contains a double meaning. We have been interested in two related themes – we have been concerned to change the ways in which the urban is theorized to include a culturalist perspective in order to reduce the demonization of the city and of the urban working classes, that frequently occurs. We have also been concerned with some of the ways that education in urban schools can be changed and is changing.

Many of the studies that deal with the urban setting and urban education more specifically, understandably focus on the structural and material realities of urbanization. Frequently, urban education reports, particularly those produced by the UK governments, focus on issues of poverty and deprivation. Indeed, many of the policies that are targeted at urban communities include a lexicon of exclusion reflected in words like 'disadvantage' and 'deprivation'. While it is critically important to understand (and change) the oppressive structural and material experiences that influence urban education, is it not just as important to value the cultural dimensions of urban life? Indeed, a fuller appreciation of, and respect for, the richness, ambivalences, excitement, dreams and desires that are wrapped up with living in the city could make an appreciable contribution to the curriculum and pedagogy of the urban classroom (Freire, 1972; Black, 2000). If an appreciation of the urban context was to be attempted in a more integrated and holistic manner, then perhaps teachers would be able to draw on the cultural knowledge of children and students to form the basis of a critical pedagogy (Giroux, 2001; Apple and Beane, 2007). One possibility that might emerge would be the prospect of 'doing school differently'; what has been done so far hasn't been working fairly or justly for working-class children and their families (Fine and Weis, 2003; Maddock et al., 2007; te Riele, 2009).

Some time ago, Grace (1984: 109) pointed out that

> The weakness of the field of urban education has been its detachment from the theoretical debates and developments of urban social theory. Such detachment has restricted its ability to formulate a comprehensive agenda for study.

To this we would add, 'and a comprehensive agenda for action'. At the very least, urban schools need sustained additional resources in order to create and sustain a buffer against the wider economic conditions that may be limiting their chances of success. Breakfast programmes, extended days, homework classes, support for parents and carers, additional mentors and counsellors, easy access to health care and advice – all these sorts of additional provisions can help support urban school communities. But they have been tried. And while they make a small difference, they do nothing to alter the status quo in a class-driven meritocratic system (Bratlinger, 2003). What is needed is a more radical set of approaches that can subvert this way of doing school. The urban school should serve as a local resource for the local community where information and library-based resources are more widely accessed. There should be stronger attempts to produce people who can author their own lives more powerfully through accessing a critical and risk-taking pedagogy (Giroux, 1988). But should not an agenda for action also incorporate a wider ethical and political perspective that impacts contemporary urban education? Rather than seeing urban schools as isolated from their communities, or as needing to 'immunize' children against the complexities of urban living, more complex spatial understandings of these schools as 'in' and 'of' their communities could provide an alternative way forward. The impact of living in poor housing and having reduced access to welfare provision, for example, needs recognition and proper and sustained reforms in any meaningful attempt to provide a (really useful) urban education (Johnson, 1976).

Working with parents and constructing democratic approaches towards learning and teaching in schools, in ways that respect what children and young people already know and bring with them, might hold out more promise for a better way ahead in urban education (Kincheloe and Hayes, 2007). Grace (2007: 972) has pointed out, correctly in our view, that there are 'resources for hope' because of the 'relative improvements in the performance of some inner-city schools'. Nevertheless, he also raises a central point: 'if this is what can be accomplished in existing circumstances, what might be achieved if these circumstances were radically changed?' As Bernstein (1970) argued some time ago, 'Education cannot compensate for society', but schools are contradictory spaces where students and teachers can subvert and resist some of the prevailing objectives if they are active, critical risk takers.

In this book, we have recognized the potential for change that is offered by interventions such as critical pedagogy, or creative applications of new and emergent technologies (although there are dangers in seeing these as 'magic bullets' that will solve every problem). What we have suggested is that an approach that starts from a different perspective might provide an engaging and relevant curriculum without displacing core skills. This is not an either/or matter. As Corson (1998: 126) has written, 'instead of changing children from diverse backgrounds in some way, to suit the school, I prefer to think about changing the forms of education that undervalue the things that many children bring to school with them'. In Archer et al.'s (2010) terms, urban schools need to think about the three Rs, namely 'respect, reciprocity and relevance'.

Changing how the urban is understood by replacing the 'dark city' with a contextualized approach that values its richness and diversity as well as changing how urban education is expressed in terms of a critical pedagogy are central in rethinking the urban in theory and practice. Despite the policies of neo-liberalism and an economistic approach towards education, 'Another world is possible. Because of that, another school is possible – and very necessary' (Wrigley, 2006: 10).

Justice, hope and vision

No change is possible without hope – hope for social justice and social transformation. As Halpin (2003) claims, education is fundamentally tied up with hope, in terms of improving educational processes. Some time ago Grace (1994) argued that urban theory and urban education needed to be complemented by what he termed 'complex hope' (see also Thrupp and Tomlinson, 2005). By this, he was referring to 'an optimism of the will that recognises the historical and structural difficulties that have to be overcome' (Grace, 1994: 57). More recently, Grace (2007: 971) has qualified what he meant by complex hope as involving 'a commitment to working for wider socio-political and cultural change . . . a praxis of the common good and of serious social justice'. But, he argues, sometimes, those most able to know what the situation is like in urban schools, are sidelined from expressing their views. For example, Jones (2003: 162) has claimed that in terms of the 'management and direction of schools', teachers have become 'subordinate'. 'Being political' is not seen as desirable or acceptable for teachers and other public sector workers. Instead, 'those who know least', media pundits and the constantly revolving government ministers 'achieve maximum publicity for their accounts' (Grace, 2007: 971) but provide a rhetoric that 'lack (s) depth and authenticity' (Thrupp and Tomlinson, 2005: 551). Rather, it is necessary to 'recognise the impact of teaching, the politics of teaching and the hope of teaching' (Edgoose, 2009: 121) – the possibility of doing things differently.

Instead of 'more of the same', that is, an education system aligned to the alleged needs of a global neo-liberal market place, that serves the middle classes well and the working classes much less favourably, there is a powerful need to create and extend 'a public education designed to express and create the values of an educated democracy and a common culture' (Williams, 1973: 179). There needs to be a concerted political and moral challenge to the social injustices and inequalities that characterize the contemporary urban setting in Britain (Wilkinson and Pickett, 2009) and elsewhere (Porfilo and Malott, 2008). As Hobsbawm (2009: xx) has urged, there needs to be: 'A return to the conviction that economic growth and the affluence it brings is a means and not an end. The end is what it does to the lives, life-chances and hopes of people'.

Education provision, as it is currently constituted in many national settings, is an intensely competitive experience. It is a game if you like, where there can only be a few winners and a great many losers. All the while, the game is pronounced as being 'fair' because everyone gets the same curriculum and the same teaching. Those who have traditionally 'lost' in the game, or seem to be in danger of 'losing', get extra support to try to succeed in the game. And some of these supported children do win a few prizes. But they are the exceptions and serve to provide a pseudo-legitimacy to the game itself.

Education policy in urban settings has frequently concentrated on supporting working-class children in a game where others have advantages that are rarely acknowledged. Wrigley (2006: 66) puts it this way:

> Official advice on improving school ethos is often functionalist, as if it were only a means to an end – the road to higher test results. A genuine concern would require us to consider how we might really enrich young lives.

If we change the curriculum to take in the cultural capital of urban children, we run the risk of giving these children a curriculum that is less valued in distributing life chances. 'We must find a way for our schools to become crucibles for change. Unless we can do that, we, with our children, are trapped in a repeating violence of our own making' (Epp, 1996: 194, cited in Archer et al., 2010: 184). We need a radical restructuring of content, assessment and pedagogy if we are to make a difference to urban children in urban schools – no more tinkering at the edges (Compton-Lilly, 2009). Vested interests and powerful voices have prevailed so far – so any response has to reach beyond education policy into a new politics for justice.

As we are finishing this book, we are in the middle of what is turning out to be an unprecedented global recession/depression. One thing is evident; unfettered neo-liberalism has not worked. 'The creation of a competitive market state in which there is no level playing field for the disadvantaged to take part is not socially just, and despite a political rhetoric of social justice there is little realization of a democratic common good' (Thrupp and Tomlinson, 2005: 552). It is time for a change, in thinking, in politics and in education (Gamble, 2009). In terms of the urban settings where the majority of us now live, and in terms of how we educate our future generations, it is evident that what has gone before has not worked. The story of the urban working classes and their education is an enduring tale of some small successes, frequently against the odds, alongside a backdrop of continuing and widespread exclusion. What is needed now is not more of the same, shared out a little more equitably; what is needed is a different school for a different and better world. This is a time for new thinking and new visions. There is no more time to waste.

Further reading

Fielding, M. and Moss, P. (2010) *Radical Education and the Common School*. London: Routledge.

Kincheloe, J. L. and Hayes, K. (eds) (2007) *Teaching City Kids: Understanding and Appreciating Them.* New York and Oxford: Peter Lang.

Te Riele, K. (ed.) (2009) *Making Schools Different: Alternative Approaches to Educating Young People.* London and New York: Sage.

Wrigley, T. (2006) *Another School is Possible.* London: Bookmarks. (See in particular the second part that details innovative practice.)

Useful websites

http://www.dcsf.gov.uk/

Department for Children, Schools and Families

http://www.teachernet.gov.uk/educationoverview/currentstrategy/nationalchallenge/

National Challenge Schools

http://uei.uchicago.edu/stories/index.shtml

Urban Education Institution, University of Chicago

Bibliography

Ackroyd, P. (2001) *London the Biography*. London: Vintage.

Ainscow, M. and West, M. (eds) (2006) *Improving Urban Schools, Leadership and Collaboration*. Maidenhead: Open University Press.

Alexander, R. (2004) 'Still no pedagogy? Principle, pragmatism and compliance in primary education', *Cambridge Journal of Education*, March, 34 (1): 7–33.

Alsayyad, N. (2006) *Cinematic Urbanism. A History of the Modern from Reel to Real*. New York and London: Routledge.

Anyon, J. (1997) *Ghetto Schooling: A Political Economy of Urban Educational Reform*. Albany: SUNY.

Anyon, J. (2005) *Radical Possibilities: Public Policy, Urban Education, and a New Social Movement*. New York: Routledge.

Appadurai, A. (1996) *Modernity at Large: Cultural Dimensions in Globalization*. Minneapolis, MN: University of Minnesota Press.

Apple, M. (1990) *Ideology and Curriculum*. New York: Routledge.

Apple, M. (2003) *The State and the Politics of Knowledge*. London: RoutledgeFalmer.

Apple, M. (2006a) 'Understanding and interrupting neoliberalism and neoconservatism in education', *Pedagogies: An International Journal*, 1 (1): 21–6.

Apple, M. (2006b) *Educating the 'Right Way: Markets, Standards, God and Inequality*. New York: Routledge.

Apple, M. and Beane, J. (2007) *Democratic Schools: Lessons in Powerful Education*. Oxford: Heinemann.

Apple, M., Au, W. and Gandin, L. A. (eds) (2009) *The Routledge International Handbook of Critical Education*. New York and London: Routledge.

Archer, L. (2003) *'Race', Masculinity and Schooling: Muslim Boys and Education*. Buckingham: Open University Press.

Archer, L. and Francis, B. (2007) *Understanding Minority Ethnic Achievement. Race, Gender, Class and 'Success'*. London: Routledge.

Archer, L., Hollingworth, S. and Mendick, H. (2010) *Urban Youth and Schooling: The Experiences and Identities of Educationally 'at Risk' Young People*. Maidenhead: McGraw-Hill/Open University Press.

Association of Teachers and Lecturers (2007) *Faith Schools: Position Statement*. London: ATL. Online. Available at: <http://www.atl.org.uk/policy-and-campaigns/policies/Faith-schools.asp> (accessed 26 April 2009).

Aurigi, A. (2005) 'Competing urban visions and the shaping of the digital city', *Knowledge, Technology and Policy*, Spring, 18 (1): 12–6.

Baldock, P., Fitzgerald, D. and Kay, J. (2005) *Understanding Early Years Policy*. 2nd edn. London: Paul Chapman.

Ball, S. and Vincent, C. (2005) 'The "childcare champion"? New Labour, social justice and the childcare market', republished in E. Woods (ed.) (2008) *The Routledge Reader in Early Childhood Education*. London and New York: Routledge, pp. 195–210.

Ball, S. J. (2003) *Class Strategies and the Education Market. The Middle Classes and Social Advantage*. London and New York: RoutledgeFalmer.

Ball, S. J. (2006) *Education Policy and Social Class*. London: Routledge.

Ball, S. J. (2008) *The Education Debate*. Bristol: Policy Press.

Ball, S. J., Maguire, M. and Macrae, S. (2000) *Choice, Pathways and Transitions Post 16: New Youth, New Economies in the Global City*. London: RoutledgeFalmer.

Barber, M. (2009) *Impossible and Necessary: Are You Ready for this?* London: NESTA. Online. Available at: <www.nesta.org.uk/home/SearchForm?Search=Impossible+and+Necessary%3A+Are+You+R eady+for+This%2C+&action_results=go> (accessed 5 July 2009).

Barker, B. (2008) 'School reform policy in England since 1988: relentless pursuit of the unattainable', *Journal of Education Policy*, 23 (6): 669–84.

Baronov, D. (2006) 'Globalisation and Urban Education', in J. Kincheloe, K. Hayes, K. Rose and P. Anderson (eds) *The Praeger Handbook of Urban Education (vol 2)*. Westport, CT: Greenwood Press, pp. 12–18.

Bartley, P. (1999) *Prostitution: Prevention and Reform in England 1860–1914*. London: Routledge.

British Educational Communications and Technology Agency (Becta) (2006) *ImpaCT 2: The Impact of Information and Communication Technologies on Pupil Learning and Attainment*. Coventry: Becta.

Becta (2007) *Research Report: Impact of ICT in Schools: A Landscape Review*. Coventry: Becta.

Becta (2008a) *Extending Opportunity: Final Report of the Minister's Taskforce on Home Access to Technology*. Online. Available at: <*partners.becta.org.uk/upload-dir/.../page.../home_access_report. pdf*> *(accessed 13 July 2009)*.

Becta (2008b) ICT Excellence Awards 2008 Best Whole School National Winner Secondary. Online. Available at: <http://awards.becta.org.uk/display.cfm?resID=38680> (accessed 7 April 2009).

Becta (2009a) *Harnessing Technology for Next Generation Learning Children, Schools and Families Implementation Plan 2009–2012*. Coventry: Becta.

Becta (2009b) First Families Receive Computers under Home Access Programme Press Release. Online. Available at: <http://news.becta.org.uk/display.cfm?resID=39686> (accessed 7 April 2009).

Belchem, J. (2007) *Irish, Catholic and Scouse: The History of the Liverpool-Irish, 1800–1939*. Liverpool: University of Liverpool Press.

Bell, D. (2003) 'Education Action Zones and Excellence in Cities', *Education Review*, 17 (1): 10–15.

Bell, D. and Haddour, A. (2000) 'What We Talk about When We Talk about the City', in D. Ball and A. Haddour (eds) *City Visions, Harlow*. Essex: Pearson Books, pp. 1–11.

Benton, G. and Gomez, E. T. (2007) *The Chinese in Britain, 1800–Present. Economy, Transnationalism, Identity*. London: Palgrave Macmillan.

Berkeley, R. (2008) *Right to Divide? Faith Schools and Community Cohesion*. London: Runnymede Trust. Online. Available at: <www.runnymedetrust.org/uploads/publications/.../RightToDivide-2008.pdf> (accessed 14 April 2008).

Bernstein, B. (1970) 'Education cannot compensate for society', *New Society (London)*, 15 (387): 344–7.

Bershady, H. (2007) 'Detectives stories and city life, society, mobility and migration', *Society*, 44 (5): 70–6.

Black, M. (2000) 'Using your city as a multicultural classroom', *Teaching Education*, 11 (3): 343–51.

Blair, M. (2001) *Why Pick On Me? School Exclusion and Black Youth*. Stoke-on-Trent: Trentham Books.

Blanden, J., Gregg, P. and Machin, S. (2005) *Intergenerational Mobility in Europe and North America: A Report Supported by the Sutton Trust*. Online. Available at: <http://www.suttontrust.com/reports/mainreport.pdf> (accessed 10 May 2009).

Blanden, J. and Machin, S. (2007) *Recent Changes in Intergenerational Mobility in Britain, Report for the Sutton Trust*. Online. Available at: <http://www.suttontrust.com/reports/mainreport.pdf> (accessed 9 April 2009).

Bodnar, J. (2007) *Dual Cities, Globalisation and Uneven Development, in Sociological Association*, TBA, New York, unpublished manuscript, Online. Available at: <http://www.allacademic.com/meta/p_mla_apa_research_citation/1/8/4/5/0/p184503> (accessed 02 March 09).

Bondi, L. (1993) 'Locating Identity Politics', in M. Keith. and S. Pile (eds) *Place and the Politics of Identity*. London: Routledge, pp. 84–102.

Bondi, L. (1998) 'Sexing the City', in R. Fincher and J. M. Jacobs (eds) *Cities of Difference*. New York and London: The Guilford Press, pp. 177–200.

Bosely, S. (2008) 'Sure Start success in helping poor children of poor families hailed', *The Guardian*, 7 November, p. 12.

Bourdieu, P. (1977) *Outline of a Theory of Practice*. Cambridge: Cambridge University Press.

Bourdieu, P. (2007) 'The Forms of Capital', in A. R. Sadovnik (ed.) *Sociology of Education: A Critical Reader*. Abingdon: Routledge, pp. 83–96.

Bourdieu, P. and Passeron, J.-C. (1979) *Reproduction in Education, Society and Culture*. London: Sage.

Brandom, A. M., Poole, M. and Wright, A. (2007) 'Spiritual Education', in J. Dillon and M. Maguire. (eds) *Becoming a Teacher. Issues in Secondary Education*. Maidenhead: McGraw-Hill Open University Press, pp. 280–91.

Bratlinger, E. (2003) *Dividing Classes. How the Middle Class Negotiates and Rationalizes School*. New York and London: RoutledgeFalmer.

Brehony, K. (2000) 'English Revisionist Froebelians and the Schooling of the Urban Poor', in M. Hilton and P. Hirsch (eds) *Practical Visionaries: Women, Education and Social Progress 1790–1930*. Harlow: Pearson Education Ltd, pp. 183–99.

Bridge, G. (2005) *Reason in the City of Difference. Pragmatism, Communicative Action and Contemporary Urbanism*. London and New York: Routledge.

Brighouse, T. and Fullick, L. (eds) (2007) *Education in a Global City*. London: Institute of Education.

Brown, M. P. (2000) *Closet Space: Geographies of Metaphor from the Body to the Globe*. London: Routledge.

Brown, P. and Lauder, H. (1996) 'Education, globalisation and economic development', *Journal of Education Policy*, 11(1): 1–25, in S. Ball (ed.) (2004) *The RoutledgeFalmer Reader in Sociology of Education*. New York: RoutledgeFalmer.

Burn, E. (2000a) 'We all count', *Primary Teaching Studies*, 11 (2): 10–14.

Burn, E. (2000b) 'You won't want to get your hands dirty: An Early Years teacher reflecting on her training experience', *Education and Social Justice*, Autumn, 3 (1): 59–64.

Burn, E. (2000c) 'Out of Class', Paper presented at British Educational Research Association Conference. University of Cardiff. 7–9 September.

Burn, E. (2001) 'Battling through the system', *Journal of Inclusive Education*, 5 (1): 85–92.

Burn, E. (2005a) 'I sat up proud', Paper presented to *Discourse, Power and Resistance Conference*. Manchester Metropolitan University. 11–14 April.

Burn, E. (2005b) 'Constructing the male primary school teacher', unpublished PhD, London Metropolitan University.

Burrows, R. (1997) 'Cyberpunk as social theory: William Gibson and the Sociological Imagination', in S. Westwood. and J. Williams (eds) *Imagining Cities*. London: Routledge, pp. 235–48.

Business Week (2005) *E-society: My World Is Cyworld*. Online. Available at: <http://www.businessweek.com/magazine/content/05_39/b3952405.htm> (accessed 29 April 09).

Byrne, D. (2005) *Social Exclusion*. Berkshire: Open University Press.

Byrne, D. S. (2001) *Understanding the Urban*. Houndmills, Basingstoke, Hampshire: Palgrave.

Cadwell, L. B. (2002) *Bringing Learning to Life: A Reggio Approach to Early Childhood Education*. New York: Teachers College Press.

Cairns, J. (2009) *Faith Schools, and Society: Civilizing the Debate*. London: Continuum.

Cameron, C., Moss, P. and Owen, C. (1999) *Men in the Nursery*. London: Sage.

Cantle, T. (2001) *Community Cohesion: A Report of the Independent Review Team*. London: Home Office.

Carr-Chellman, A. (ed.) (2005) *Global Perspectives on E-learning: Rhetoric and Reality*. London: Sage.

Carr-Chellman, A. (ed.) (2005) 'The New Frontier: Web-Based Education in the US Culture', in *Global Perspectives on E-Learning: Rhetoric and Reality*. London: Sage, pp. 145–59.

Carroll-Miranda, J. (2006) 'Education in a Globalized Society: Over Five Centuries, the Colonial Struggle Continues', in J. Kincheloe, K. Hayes, K. Rose and P. Anderson (eds) *The Praeger Handbook of Urban Education Volume 2*. Westport, CT: Greenwood Press, pp. 357–66.

Casella, R. (2006) 'The Militarized Zone', in J. Kincheloe, K. Hayes, K. Rose and P. Anderson (eds) *The Praeger Handbook of Urban Education Volume 1*. Westport, CT: Greenwood Press, pp. 10–19.

Castells, M. (1972) *The Urban Question*. London: Edward Arnold.

Castells, M. (1977) *The Urban Question: A Marxist Approach*. London: Edward Arnold.

Castells, M. (1996) *The Rise of the Network Society*. London: Blackwell.

Castells, M. (1998) *End of Millennium*. Malden, MA, and Oxford: Blackwell.

Castells, M. (1999) 'Flows, Networks, and Identities: A Critical Theory of the Information Society', in M. Castells, R. Flecha, P. Freire, H. Giroux, D. Macedo and P. Willis (eds) *Critical Education in the New Information Age*. Maryland: Rowman and Littlefield Publishers, pp. 37–64.

Castells, M. (2000) *End of Millennium. Volume 3. The Information Age: Economy, society and Culture*. 2nd edn. Oxford: Blackwell.

Castells, M. (2001) *The Internet Galaxy. Reflections on the Internet, Business and Society*. Oxford: Oxford University Press.

Castells, M. (2002) 'An Introduction to the Information Age', in G. Bridge and S. Watson (eds) *The Blackwell City Reader*. Oxford: Blackwell Publishing, pp. 125–34.

Centre for Public Policy Research (CPPR) (2002) 'Faith-based schooling and the invisible effects of 11 September 2001: the view from England', *Discourse*, 23 (3): 309–17.

Cerny, P. G. and Evans, M. (2004) 'Globalisation and public policy under New Labour', *Policy Studies*, 25 (1): 51–65.

Charlesworth, V. (2009) *Critical Skills in the Early Years*. London: Network Continuum Education.

Chatterton, P. and Hollands, R. (2003) *Urban Nightscapes, Youth Cultures, Pleasure Spaces and Corporate Power*. London: Routledge.

Chen, M. (2000) 'Internet Content Should Reflect Children's Diversity of Needs and Interests, in D. Gordon (ed.) *The Digital Classroom: How technology is changing the way we teach and learn*. Cambridge, MA: The Harvard Education Letter, pp. 151–3.

Chowdry, H., Crawford, C. and Goodman, I. (2009) *Drivers and Barriers to Educational Success. Evidence from the Longitudinal Study of Young People in England. Research Report DCSF-RR 102*. London: Institute for Fiscal Studies.

Cicirelli, V. G. (1972) 'Education Models for the Disadvantaged', in J. Raynor and E. Harris (eds) *Schooling in the City*. Glasgow: Ward Lock Educational in association with the Open University Press, pp. 253–62.

Cinar, A. and Bender, T. (2007) 'The City: Experience, Imagination and Place', in A. Cinar and T. Bender (eds) *Urban Imaginaries. Locating the Modern City*. Minneapolis, MN, and London: University of Minnesota Press, pp. xi–xxvi.

Clarke, D. B. (ed.) (1997) *The Cinematic City*. London and New York: Routledge.

Clarke, K. (1985) 'Public and Private Children: Infant Education in the 1820s and 1830s', in C. Steedman, C. Urwin and V. Walkerdine. (eds) *Language, Gender and Childhood*. London: Routledge & Kegan Paul, pp. 74–87.

Clay, M. M. (1982) *Observing Young Readers*. New Hampshire: Heinemann.

Cohen, R. and Kennedy, P. (2007) *Global Sociology*. 2nd edn. Basingstoke: Palgrave.

Coleman, J. S. (1990) *Foundations of Social Theory*. Cambridge, MA: The Belknap Press of Harvard University Press.

Coles, M. I. (2008) *Every Muslim Child Matters: Practical Guidance for Schools and Children's Services*. Oakhill, Virginia: Trentham.

Colley, H. (2003) *Mentoring for Social Inclusion: A Critical Approach to Nurturing Mentoring Relationships*. London and New York: RoutledgeFalmer.

Collins, A. (ed.) (2006) *Cities of Pleasure: Sex and the Urban Socialscape*, London and New York: Routledge.

Compton-Lilly, C. (ed.) (2009) *Breaking the Silence: Recognizing the Social and Cultural Resources Students Bring to the Classroom*, Newark, DE: International Reading Association.

Connolly, P. (1998) *Racism, Gender Identities and Young Children*. London: Routledge.

Cook, J., Pachler, N. and Bradley, C. (2008) 'Bridging the Gap? Mobile Phones at the Interface Between Informal and Formal Learning', *Journal of the Research Center for Educational Technology*,

Spring, 4(1), Online. Available at: <http:// www.rcetj.org.PrintArticle.aspx?type=prn&id=87827> (accessed 02 May 2008).

Corson, D. (1998) *Changing Education for Diversity*. Buckingham: Open University Press.

Crace, J. (2008) 'Long division', *Education Guardian*, 11 November, p. 1.

Cressey, P. G. (1932) *The Taxi-Dance Hall: A Sociological Study in Commercialized Recreation and City Life*. Chicago, IL: University of Chicago Press.

Cribb, A. and Gewirtz, S. (2003) 'Towards a Sociology of Just Practices. An Analysis of Plural Conceptions of Justice', in C. Vincent (ed.) (2003) *Social Justice, Education and Identity*. London and New York: RoutledgeFalmer, pp. 15–29.

Crozier, G. and Reay, D. (2005) *Activating Participation: Parents and Teachers Working towards Partnership*. Stoke on Trent: Trentham.

Cuban, L. (2001) *Oversold and Underused: Computers in the Classroom*. Cambridge, MA, and London: Harvard University Press.

Cunningham, P. (2000) 'The Montessori Phenomenon: Gender and Internationalism in Early Twentieth-Century Innovation', in M. Hilton and P. Hirsch (eds) *Practical Visionaries: Women, Education and Social Progress 1790–1930*. Harlow: Pearson Education Ltd, pp. 203–20.

Curtis, P. (2007a) 'England plunges in rankings for reading', *The Guardian*, Thursday, 29 November 2007. Online. Available at: <http://www.guardian.co.uk/uk/2007/nov/29/schools.booksnews> (accessed 30 November 2007).

Curtis, P. (2007b) '"Failing" school reforms put Labour under pressure', *The Guardian*, 13 November 2007. Online. Available at: <http://www.guardian.co.uk/uk/2007/nov/13/schools.newschools> (accessed 30 November 2007).

Curtis, S. J. (1967) *History of Education in Great Britain*. 7th edn. London: University Tutorial Press.

Davidson, M., del, G. and Yancy, G. (eds) (2009) *Critical Perspectives on Bell Hooks*. New York: Routledge.

Davin, A. (1996) *Growing Up Poor*. London: Rivers Oram Press.

Davis, M. (1990) *City of Quartz: Excavating the Future in Los Angeles*. London: Vintage Books.

de Freitas, S. (2008) *Serious Virtual Worlds: A Scoping Study*. Serious Games Institute. Available at: <www.jisc.ac.uk/publications/publications/seriousvirtualworldsreport.aspx.> (accessed 30 September 2009).

Department for Children, Schools and Families (DCSF) (2007a) *Guidance on the Duty to Promote Community Cohesion*. London: Department for Children, Schools and Families.

Department for Children, Schools and Families (DCSF) (2007b) *The Children's Plan*. Online. Available at: <http://www.dcsf.gov.uk/childrensplan/downloads/The_Childrens_Plan.pdf> (accessed 12 December 2007).

Department for Children, Schools and Families (DCSF) (2008) *Statutory Framework for the Early Years Foundation Stage Framework*. Nottingham: DCSF Publications.

Department for Children, Schools and Families (DCSF) *The City Challenge*. Online. Available at: <http://www.dcsf.gov.uk/citychallenge/london.shtml> (accessed 10 October 2008).

Department for Children, Schools and Families (DCSF) (2009) *Your Child, Your Schools, Our Future: Building a 21st Century School System (Cm. 7588)*. London: The Stationery Office.

Department for Culture Media and Sport (DCMS) (2009) *Digital Britain: The Final Report*. London: HMSO.

Department for Education and Employment (DfEE) (1995) *Grants for Education Support and Training. Raising Standards in Inner City Schools 1992–1995*. London: DFEE.

Department for Education and Employment (DfEE) (1997a) *The Implementation of the National Literacy Strategy*. London: DfEE.

Department for Education and Employment (DfEE) (1997b) *Excellence in Schools*, (Cmnd 3681). London: HMSO.

Department for Education and Employment (DfEE) (1999a) *Excellence in Cities*. Nottingham: DfEE Publications.

Department for Education and Employment (DfEE) (1999b) *Sure Start: A Guide for trailblazers*. London: The Stationary Office.

Department for Education and Skills (DfES) (1997) *Meeting the Childcare Challenge: The National Childcare Strategy*. London: Her Majesty's Stationary Office.

Department for Education and Skills (DfES) (2001) *Schools Building on Success*. London: DfES Publications.

Department for Education and Skills (DfES) (2002) *A Primary Strategy 2002–2007*. London: DfES Primary Education Programme Board, May.

Department for Education and Skills (DfES) (2004) *Five Year Strategy for Children and Learners*. Online. Available at: <http://www.dfes.gov.uk/publications/5yearstrategy> (accessed 4 June 2006).

Department for Education and Skills (DfES) (2005) *Harnessing Technology: Transforming Learning and Children's Services*. Nottingham: DfES Publications.

Department for Education and Skills (DfES) (2006a) *Schools Facing Challenging Circumstances*. Online. Available at: <http://www.standards.dfes.gov.uk/sie/si/SfCC/> (accessed 18 June 2006).

Digital Inclusion: Communities and neighbourhoods. Online. Available at: <http://www.communities. gov.uk/communities/digitalinclusion/> (accessed 18 June 2009).

Dobson, S. (2007) 'Urban Pedagogy: A Challenge for the 21st Century', in M. Reiss, R. DePalma and E. Atkinson (eds) *Marginality and Difference in Education and Beyond*. Stoke on Trent: Trentham Books, pp. 165–78.

Dodge, M., Smith, A. and Doyle, S. (1997) 'Urban science', *GIS Europe*, October, 6 (10): 26–9. Online. Available at: <http://www.casa.ucl.ac.uk/martin/virtual_cities.html> (accessed 02 March 2009).

Donald, J. (1992) 'Metropolis: The City as Text', in R. Bocock and K. Thompson (eds) *Social and Cultural Forms of Modernity*. Cambridge: Polity Press, pp. 417–61.

Dorling, D., Rigby, J., Wheeler, B., Ballas, D., Thomas, B. and Lupton, R. (2007) *Poverty, Wealth and Place in Britain 1968 to 2005*. Cambridge: Polity Press.

Du Gay, P., Evan, J. and Redman, P. (eds) (2002) *Identity: A Reader*. London: Sage.

Duncan-Andrade, J. and Morrell, E. (2007) 'Critical Pedagogy and Popular Culture in an Urban Secondary English Classroom', in J. Kincheloe and P. McLaren (eds) *Critical Pedagogy: Where Are We Now?* New York: Peter Lang, pp. 183–98.

Ecclestone, K. (2004) 'From Freire to Fear: The Rest of Therapeutic Pedagogy in Post-16 Education', in J. Satterthwaite, E. Atkinson and W. Martin (eds) *The Disciplining of Education*. Stoke-on-Trent: Trentham Books, pp. 117–36.

Edgoose, J. (2009) 'Radical hope and teaching: learning political agency from the politically disenfranchised', *Educational Theory*, 59 (1): 105–21.

Edwards, B. (1974) *The Burston School Strike.* London: Lawrence and Wishart.

e-Learning Foundation (2006) *Annual Review 2005–2006.* Leatherhead: e-Learning Foundation.

Emden, C., Keen, C. and Midgley, D. (eds) (2006) *The Art of Urban Living. Imagining the City, Vol. 1.* Oxford: Peter Lang.

Engels, F. (1892) *The Condition of the Working-Class in England in 1844.* London: Swan Sonnenschein & Co.

Ennals, P. (2004) *Child Poverty and Education.* London: National Children's Bureau.

Epstein, D., Hewitt, R., Leonard, D., Mauthner, M. and Watkins, C. (2003) 'Avoiding the issue: homophobia, school policies and identities in secondary schools', in Vincent, C. (ed.) *Social Justice, Education and Identity.* London: RoutledgeFalmer, pp. 120–36.

Ferrell, J. (1993) *Crimes of Style: Urban Graffiti and the Politics of Criminality.* New York: Garland.

Fielding, M. and Moss, P. (2010) *Radical Education and the Common School,* London: Routledge.

Fincher, R. and Jacobs, J. (eds) (1998) *Cities of Difference.* New York: Guilford.

Fine, M. and Weis, L. (2003) *Silenced Voices and Extraordinary Conversations: Re-Imagining Schools.* New York: Teachers College Press.

Fishman, W. (1988) *East End 1888: A Year in a London Borough among the Labouring Poor.* London: Duckworth.

Fitz, J., Davies, B. and Evans, J. (2006) *Educational Policy and Social Reproduction: Class Inscription and Symbolic Control.* Abingdon: Routledge.

Fitzpatrick, S. and Conway, P. (2005) 'Online learning and differential participation in a democratic society: Ireland as a case study', in A. Carr-Chellman (ed.) *Global Perspectives on E-learning: Rhetoric and Reality.* London: Sage, pp. 71–88.

Flaherty, J., Veit-Wilson, J. and Dornan, P. (2004) *Poverty: The Facts.* London: CPAG.

Flecha, R. (1999) 'New Educational Inequalities', in M. Castells et al. (eds) *Critical Education in the New Information Age.* Lanham, MD: Rowman and Littlefield Publishers, pp. 65–82.

Foucault, M. (1978) *The Will to Knowledge.* London: Penguin.

Fraser, N. (1997) *Justice Interrupts: Critical Reflections on the 'Postsocialist' Condition.* New York and London: Routledge.

Freire, P. (1970; 1993) *Pedagogy of the Oppressed.* London: Penguin.

Freire, P. (1972) *Pedagogy of the Oppressed.* Harmondsworth: Penguin.

Freire, P. (1995) 'The Progressive Teacher', in M. de Figueiredo-Cowen and D. Gastaldo (eds) *Paulo Freire at the Institute.* Institute of Education: University of London.

Freire, P. (1996) *Letters to Christina.* New York: Routledge.

Freire, P. (1998) *Pedagogy of the Heart.* New York: Continuum.

Freire, P. (2007) *Pedagogy of Hope.* 2nd edn. New York: Continuum.

Friedland, R. and Boden, D. (eds) (1994) *Space, Time and Modernity.* London: University of California Press.

Frisby, D. (2001) *Cityscapes of Modernity. Critical Explorations.* Cambridge: Polity Press.

Fryer, P. (1984) *Staying Power: The History of Black People in Britain.* London: Pluto.

Galbraith, J. (1992) *The Culture of Contentment*. London: Sinclair-Stevenson.

Gale, T. (2001) 'Critical policy sociology: historiography, archaeology and genealogy as methods of policy analysis', *Journal of Education Policy*, 16 (5): 379–93.

Gamble, A. (2009) *The Spectre at the Feast: Capitalist Crisis and the Politics of Recession*. London: Palgrave Macmillan.

Gandin, L. (2004) 'New schools, new knowledge, new teachers: creating the citizen school in Porto Alegre, Brazil', in *Teacher Education Quarterly*, Winter, pp. 1–16.

Gandin, L. A. and Apple, M. W. (2003) 'Educating the State, democratizing knowledge: The Citizen school project in Porto Alegre, Brazil', in M. W. Apple (ed.) *The State and the Politics of Knowledge*. London: RoutledgeFalmer, pp. 193–219.

Gandin, L. A. and Fischman, G. (2006) 'Participatory democratic education: is the utopia possible? Porto Alegre's Citizen School Project', in P. Anderson, K. Hayes, D. Griffith and J. Kincheloe (eds) *Urban Education an Encyclopaedia*. Westport, CT: Greenwood Press, pp. 135–46.

Garner, R. (2008) 'Number of "inadequate" childminders doubles in a year says inspectors', *Independent*, p. 8, 27 August.

Gastaldo, D. and de Figueiredo-Cowen, M. (1995) 'Paulo Freire in the nineties: life experience and progressive education', in M. de Figueiredo-Cowen and D. Gastaldo (eds) *Paulo Freire at the Institute*. Institute of Education: University of London, pp. 1–16.

Gewirtz, S. (2001) 'Cloning the Blairs: New Labour's programme for the re-socialization of working-class parents', *Journal of Education Policy*, 16 (4): 365–78.

Gewirtz, S. (2006) 'Towards a contextualized analysis of social justice in education', *Educational Philosophy and Theory*, 38 (1): 69–81.

Giddens, A. (1985) *A Contemporary Critique of Historical Materialism*. Vol 2. The Nation-State and Violence. Cambridge: Polity Press.

Giddens, A. (1990) *The Consequences of Modernity*. Oxford: Blackwell.

Giddens, A. (1996) *Durkheim on Politics and the State*. Cambridge: Polity Press.

Giddens, A. (1999) *Runaway World: How Globalism is Reshaping Our Lives*. London: Routledge.

Giddens, A. (2007) *Europe in a Global Age*. Cambridge: Polity Press.

Gilbert, D. (1998) *The American Class Structure*. New York: Wadsworth Publishing.

Gillborn, D. (1997) 'Racism, selection, poverty and parents: New Labour, old problems?' *Journal of Education Policy*, 13 (6): 717–35.

Gillborn, D. and Mirza, H. S. (2000) *Educational Inequality: Mapping Race, Class and Gender – A Synthesis of Research Evidence*. HMI 232, London: OFSTED.

Giroux, H. A. (1988) *Teachers as Intellectuals: Toward a Critical Pedagogy of Learning*. Westport, CT: Bergin and Garvey.

Giroux, H. A. (1992) *Border Crossings: Cultural Workers and the Politics of Education*. New York: Routledge.

Giroux, H. A. (1994) *Disturbing Pleasures*. London: Routledge.

Giroux, H. A. (2001) *Theory and Resistance in Education: Towards a Pedagogy for the Opposition*, Westport, CT, and London: Bergin and Garvey.

Giroux, H. A. (2009) Education and the crisis of youth: schooling and the promise of democracy, *The Educational Forum*, 73: 8–18.

Glaeser, E. (1998) 'Are cities dying?' *Journal of Economic Perspectives*, Spring, 12 (2): 139–60.

Glass, F. (2008) 'Conflict in cities', in A. V. S. de Reuck and J. Knight (eds) *Ciba Foundation Symposium – Conflict in Society*. Online. Available at: <http://www3.interscience.wiley.com/cgi-bin/summary/119229546/SUMMARY> (accessed 5 January 2009).

Gleeson, B. (1998) 'Justice and the disabling city, in R. Fincher and J. M. Jacobs (eds) *Cities of Difference*. New York: Guilford Press, pp. 89–119.

The Global Kids Project (2006) Online. Available at: <www.globalkids.org> (accessed 29 October 2008).

Goldstrom, J. M. (1972) *Education-Elementary Education, 1780–1900*. Newton Abbot: David and Charles.

Gorard, S. (2005) 'Academies as the 'future of schooling': is this an evidence-based policy?' *Journal of Education Policy*, 20 (3): 369–78

Gorard, S. (2009) 'What are Academies the answer to?' *Journal of Education Policy*, 24 (1): 101–13.

Gottdiener, M. and Hutchison, R. (2006) *The New Urban Sociology*. Boulder, CO: Westview Press.

Grace, G. (1978) *Teachers, Ideology and Control: A Study in Urban Education*. London: Routledge and Kegan Paul.

Grace, G. (1984) 'Theorising the urban: some approaches for students of education', in Grace, G. (ed.) *Education and the City. Theory, History and Contemporary Practice*, London: Routledge and Kegan Paul, pp. 94–114.

Grace, G. (1994) *Education and the City: Theory, History and Contemporary Practice*. London: Routledge and Kegan Paul.

Grace, G. (1995) 'Theorizing social relations within urban schooling: a socio-historical analysis', in P. Atkinson, B. Davies and S. Delamont (eds), *Discourse and Reproduction: Essays in Honour of Basil Bernstein*. Cresskill, NJ: Hampton Press, pp. 209–28.

Grace, G. (2001) 'The State and Catholic Schooling in England and Wales. Politics, ideology and mission integrity', *Oxford Review of Education*, 24 (4): 489–500.

Grace, G. (2007) 'Urban education theory revisited: from the urban question to end of millennium', in W. T. Pink and G. W. Noblit (eds) *International Handbook of Urban Education*. London and New York: Springer, pp. 959–78.

Graham, S. and Aurigi, A. (1997) 'Urbanising cyberspace? The nature and potential of the virtual cities movement', *City*, 7: 18–40.

Gramsci, A. (1968) *Prison Notebooks*. London: Lawrence and Wishart.

Great Britain. Treasury (2003) *Every Child Matters*. Norwich: Stationery Office.

Greed, C. (1987) 'Women and the Built Environment'. Unpublished paper, Working papers in Urban Education, Centre for Educational Studies, King's College London.

Greed, C. (1994) *Women and Planning: Creating Gendered Realities*. London and New York: Routledge.

Greenfield, A. (2006) *Everyware: The Dawning Age of Ubiquitous Computing (Voices That Matter)*. Berkeley, CA: New Riders Publishing.

Groenke, S. L. and Amos Hatch, J. (eds) (2009) *Critical Pedagogy and Teacher Education in the Neoliberal Era: Small Openings*. Dordrecht: Springer.

Gulson, K. (2005) 'Renovating educational identities: policy, space and urban renewal', *Journal of Education Policy*, 20 (2): 141–58.

Hall, C. (1995) *White, Male and Middle Class.* Cambridge: Polity Press.

Hall, S. (1977) 'Education and the crisis of the urban school', in J. Raynor and E. Harris (eds) *Schooling the City.* Glasgow: Ward Lock in association with The Open University, pp. 7–17.

Halpin, D. (2003) *Hope and Education: The Role of the Utopian Imagination.* London and New York: RoutledgeFalmer.

Halsey, A. H., Heath, A. F. and Ridge, J. M. (1980) *Origins and Destinations: Family, Class, and Education in Modern Britain.* Oxford: Clarendon Press.

Halstead, J. M. and McLaughlin, T. (2005) 'Are faith schools divisive?' in R. Gardner, J. Cairns and D. Lawton, (eds), *Faith Schools: Consensus or Conflict?* London: Routledge Falmer, pp. 61–73.

Hamnett, C. (2003) *Unequal City. London in the Global Arena.* London and New York: Routledge.

Harris, J. (1993) *Private Lives, Public Spirit: Britain 1870–1914.* London: Penguin.

Harvey, D. (1973) *Social Justice and the City.* London: Edward Arnold.

Harvey, D. (1989a) *The Urban Experience,* Oxford: Basil Blackwell.

Harvey, D. (1989b) *The Condition of Post Modernity: An Enquiry into the Origins of Cultural Change.* Oxford: Basil Blackwell.

Hellawell, S. (2001) *Beyond Access ICT and Social Inclusion.* London: The Fabian Society.

Helsper, E. (2008) *Digital Exclusion: An Analysis of Social Disadvantage and the Information Society.* Department for Communities and Local Government, October. London: HMSO.

Hess, F. and Leal, D. (1999) 'Computer-assisted learning in urban classrooms: the impact of politics, race and class', *Urban Education,* 34 (3): 370–88.

Hills, J., Seflint, T. and Stewart, K. (eds) (2009) *Towards a More Equal Society? Poverty, Inequality and Policy since 1997.* Bristol: Policy Press.

Hirsch, D. (2007) *Chicken and Egg: Child Poverty and Educational Inequalities.* Policy Briefing, London: CPAG. Online. Available at: <http://www.cpag.org.uk/campaigns/education/Education-Briefing120907.pdf.> (accessed 11 November 2007).

Hobsbawm, E. (2009) 'Socialism has failed. Now capitalism is bankrupt. So what comes next?' *The Guardian,* Friday, 10 April 2009. Online. Available at: <http://www.guardian.co.uk/commentisfree/2009/apr/10/financial-crisis-capitalism-socialism-alternatives> (accessed 11 July 2009).

Hollingworth, S., Allen, K., Hutchings, M., Kuyok, K. and Williams, K. (2008) *Technology and School Improvement: Reducing Social Inequity with Technology?* Online. Available at: <http://www.londonmet.ac.uk/research-units/ipse/research-projects/completed-projects/p76.cfm> (accessed 20 November 2008).

hooks, b. (1984) *Feminist Theory: From Margin to Center.* Boston, MA: South End Press.

hooks, b. (1989) *Talking Back.* Boston, MA: South End Press.

hooks, b. (1994) *Teaching to Transgress.* London: Routledge.

hooks, b. (2000) *Where We Stand: Class Matters.* London: Routledge.

House of Commons Children, Schools and Families Select Committee (2008) *HC213 -1 Minutes of Evidence taken before the Children, Schools and Families Committee,* 9 January 2008.

Howard, M. (2004) *Tax Credits: One Year On.* London: CPAG.

Husen, T. (1974) *The Learning Society.* London, Methuen.

Hutchins, R. (1970) *The Learning Society*. Harmondsworth: Penguin.

Huxley, A. (1932) *Brave New World*. London: Chatto and Windus.

Ishida, T. (2000) 'Understanding digital cities', in T. Ishida and K. Ishister (eds) *Digital Cities*. Berlin: Springer, pp. 7–17.

Iske, S., Klein, A., Kutscher, N. and Hans-Uwe, O. (2008) 'Young people's Internet use and its significance for informal education and social participation', *Technology, Pedagogy and Education*, July, 17 (2): 131–41.

Jackson, K. (2007) *Crabgrass Frontier: The Suburbanization of the United States*, New York: Oxford University Press.

Jacobs, J. M. and Fincher, R. (1998) 'Introduction', in R. Fincher and J. M. Jacobs, (eds) *Cities of Difference*. New York and London: The Guilford Press, pp. 1–25.

James, O. (1998) *Britain on the Couch: Why We're Unhappier Compared with 1950, Despite Being richer – A Treatment for the Low-serotonin Society*. London: Arrow Books Ltd.

Jameson, F. (1991) *Postmodernism, or, the Cultural Logic of Late Capitalism (Post-Contemporary Interventions)*. Durham, NC: Duke University Press.

Jarvis, P. (2000) 'Globalisation, the learning society and comparative education', *Comparative Education*, 36 (3): 343–55.

Jayne, M. (2006) *Cities and Consumption*. London: Routledge.

Jia Qi, J. (2005) 'The gap between E-learning availability and E-learning industry development in Taiwan', in A. Carr-Chellman (ed.) *Global Perspectives on E-learning: Rhetoric and Reality*. London: Sage, pp. 33–51.

JISC (2007) *In their own words: Exploring the learner's perspective on e-learning*. HEFCE.

Johnson, M. (1999) *Failing School, Failing City. The Reality of Inner City Education*. London: Jon Carpenter.

Johnson, R. (1976) 'Notes on the schooling of the English working class 1780–1850', in R. Dale, G. Esland and M. MacDonald. (eds) *Schooling and Capitalism. A Sociological Reader*. London: Routledge and Kegan Paul, pp. 44–54.

Jones, C. and Novak. T. (1999) *Poverty, Welfare and the Disciplinary State*. London, New York: Routledge.

Jones, K. (2003) *Education in Britain. 1944 to the Present*. Cambridge: Polity Press.

Judge, H. (2001) 'Faith-based Schools and State Funding: a partial argument', *Oxford Review of Education*, 27 (4): 463–74.

Kaplan, M. (2005) *Sodom on the Thames: Sex, Love, and Scandal in Wilde Times*. Ithaca, NY: Cornell University Press.

Kassem, D. and Murphy, L. (2009) 'Faith schools: diversity or division', in D. Kassem and D. Garrett (eds) (2009) *Exploring Key Issues in Education*. London: Continuum, pp. 69–82.

Kendall, L., O'Donnell, L., Golden, S., Ridley, K., Machin, S., Rutt, S., McNally, S., Schagen, L., Meghir, C., Stoney, S., Morros, M., West, A. and Noden, P. (2005) *Excellence in Cities: The National Evaluation of a Policy to Raise Standards in Urban Schools 2000–2003*. DfES Research Report, Nottingham: DfES Publications. Online. Available at: <http://www.dfes.gov.uk/research/data/uploadfiles/RR675A.pdf> (accessed 10 April 2009).

Kenyon, S. (2006) 'Reshaping patterns of mobility and exclusion? The impact of virtual mobility upon accessibility, mobility and social exclusion', in M. Sheller. and J. Urry (eds) *Mobile Technologies of the City*. London: Routledge, pp. 102–20.

Kerrey, B. and Isakson, J. (2000) 'The Power of the Internet for Learning. Report on the Web-Based Education Commission to the President and the Congress of the U.S', in Microsoft Education (2008) *School of the Future: Understand the vision*. Microsoft Corporation.

Kershen, A. J. (2005) *Strangers, Aliens and Asians: Huguenots, Jews and Bangladeshis in Spitalfields 1660–2000*. London: Routledge.

Kincheloe, J. L. and Hayes, K. (eds) (2007) *Teaching City Kids: Understanding and Appreciating Them*. New York, Oxford: Peter Lang.

Kohl, H. (1998) *The Discipline of Hope*. New York: Simon and Schuster.

Kohn, A. (1998) 'Only for *my* kid: how privileged parents undermine school reform', *Phi Delta Kappa*, April, pp. 569–76.

Kruger, J. and Chawla, L. (2002) 'We Know something someone doesn't know: children speak out on local conditions in Johannesburg', in *Environment and Urbanization*, October, 14 (2): 85–96.

Lacey, C. (1970) *Hightown Grammar: The School as a Social System*. Manchester: Manchester University Press.

Landry, C. (2000) *The Creative City. A Toolkit for Urban Innovators*. London: Earthscan Publication.

Lauder, H., Brown, P., Dillabough, J. and Halsey, A. (2006) 'Introduction: the prospects of education: individualization, globalization, and social change', in H. Lauder, P. Brown, J. Dillabough and A. Halsey (eds) *Education, Globalization and Social Change*. Oxford: Oxford University Press, pp. 1–63.

Lave, J. and Wenger, E. (1998) *Communities of Practice: Learning, Meaning and Identity*. Cambridge: Cambridge University Press.

Lawton, D. and Cairns, J. (2005), 'Faith schools: some political issues and an agenda for research', in R. Gardner, J. Cairns and D. Lawton (eds) *Faith Schools: Consensus or Conflict?* London: Routledge Falmer, pp. 242–56.

Lee, J. (1987) 'Pride and prejudice: teacher, class and an inner-city infants school', in M. Lawn and G. Grace (eds) *Teachers: The Culture and Politics of Work*. Lewes: Falmer Press, 91–116.

Lee, L. (2008) 'The impact of young people's internet use on class boundaries and life trajectories', in *Sociology*, 42 (1): 137–53.

Lenhart, A., Madden, M., Macgill, A. R. and Smith, A. (2007) *Teens and Social Media*. Washington, DC: Pew Internet & American Life Project.

Lewin-Benham, A. (2005) *Possible Schools: The Reggio Approach in Urban Education*. New York: Teachers College Press.

Lipman, P. (2004) *High Stakes Education: Inequality, Globalization, and Urban School Reform*. London: RoutledgeFalmer.

Livingstone, K. (2003) *Tackling Poverty in London: A Consultation Document*. London: Greater London Authority. Online. Available at: <www.london.gov.uk/mayor/economy/docs/tackling_poverty.rtf> (accessed 24 March 2008).

Livingstone, S., Bober, M. and Helsper, E. (2005) *Inequalities and the Digital Divide in Children and Young People's Internet Use: Findings from the UK Children Go Online project*. London: LSE Research. Online. Available at: <http://eprints.lse.ac.uk/archive/00000398> (accessed 08 April 2009).

Loader, B. and Keeble, L. (2005) *Challenging the Digital Divide: A Review of Online Community Support*. York: Joseph Rowntree Foundation.

Loewen, J. (1995) *Lies My Teacher Told Me: Everything Your American History Textbook Got Wrong*. New York: Simon and Schuster.

Longworth, N. (2006) *Learning Cities, Learning Regions, Learning Communities. Lifelong Learning and Local Government*. London: Routledge.

Luke, C. and Gore, J. (1992) (eds) *Feminisms and Critical Pedagogy*. New York: Routledge.

Lupton, R. (2004) *Poverty Street: The Dynamics of Neighbourhood Decline and Renewal*. Bristol: Policy Press.

Lupton, R., Heath, N. and Salter, E. (2009) 'Education: New Labour's top priority', in J. Hills, T. Seflint and K. Stewart (eds) *Towards a More Equal Society? Poverty, Inequality and Policy since 1997*. Bristol: Policy Press, pp. 71–90.

McAdoo, M. (2000) 'The real digital divide: quality not quantity, in D. Gordon (ed.) *The Digital Classroom: How Technology is Changing the Way We Teach and Learn*. Cambridge, MA: The Harvard Education Letter, pp. 143–50.

McCann, P. and Young, F. A. (1982) *Samuel Wilderspin and the Infant School Movement*. London: Croom Helm.

McCulloch, G. (1994) *Educational Reconstruction: The 1944 Education Act and the Twenty-First Century*. Ilford: Woburn.

McCulloch, G. (2007) *Cyril Norwood and the Ideal of Secondary Education*. New York, Basingstoke: Palgrave Macmillan.

McKinney, S. J. (2008) 'Mapping the debate on faith schooling in England', in McKinney, S. J. (ed.) *Faith Schools in the Twenty-first Century*. Edinburgh: Dunedin Academic Press, pp. 1–15.

Maddock, M., Drummond, M. J., Koralek, B. and Nathan, I. (2007) 'Doing school differently: creative practitioners at work', *Education 3–13*, 35 (1): 47–58.

Maguire, M. (2008) 'Fade to grey: older women, embodied claims and attributions in English university departments of education', *Women's Studies International Forum*, 31: 474–82.

Maguire, M. (2009) 'New adulthood, youth and identity', in Te Riele, K. (eds) *Making Schools Different: Alternative Approaches to Educating Young People*. Sydney and London: Sage, 31–9.

Maguire, M. (2010) 'Globalisation, education policy and the teacher', *International Studies in Sociology of Education*, 12 (3): 261–76 (forthcoming).

Maguire, M. and Dillon, J. (2007) 'Education policy and schooling', in J. Dillon and M. Maguire (eds) *Becoming a Teacher*. Maidenhead: Open University/McGrawHill, pp. 29–41.

Maguire, M. and Pratt-Adams, S. (2009) 'Improving the English urban primary school: questions of policy', *Improving Schools*, March, 12 (1): 1–12.

Maguire, M., Wooldridge, T. and Pratt-Adams, S. (2006) *The Urban Primary School*. Maidenhead: Open University Press/McGraw-Hill.

Martin, J. and Goodman, J. (2004) *Women and Education 1800–1980.* Basingstoke: Palgrave Macmillan.

Massey, D. (1984) *Spatial Division of Labour: Social Structures and the Geography of Production.* London: Macmillan.

Massood, P. J. (2003) *Black City Cinema: African American Urban Experiences in Film.* Philadelphia, PA: Temple University Press.

Matheson, D. (2004) 'What is education'? in D. Matheson (ed.) *An Introduction to the Study of Education.* 2nd edn. London: David Fulton, pp. 1–16.

Melhuish, E. (2004) *Early Years: Progress in Developing High Quality Childcare and Early Education Accessible to All.* London: National Audit Office. Online. Available at: <http://www.nao.org.uk/publications/0304/early_years_progress.aspx> (accessed 1 August 2009).

Miles, M. (2007) *Cities and Cultures.* London and New York: Routledge.

Miles, M. and Hall, T. (eds) (2003) *Urban Futures: Critical Commentaries on Shaping the City.* London: Routledge.

Mills, C. and Gale, T. (2004) 'Parent participation in disadvantaged schools: moving beyond attributions of blame', *Australian Journal of Education,* 48 (3): 268–81.

Mingione, E. (1996) *Urban Poverty and the Underclass.* Oxford: Blackwell.

Mitchell, W. (1995) *City of Bits: Space, Place, and the Infobahn.* Cambridge, MA: MIT Press.

Mitchell, W. (2000) 'Designing the digital city', in T. Ishida and K. Ishister (eds) *Digital Cities.* Berlin: Springer, pp. 1–6.

Modood, T. (ed.) (1997) *Church, State and Religious Minorities.* London: Policy Studies Institute.

Moriarty, V. (1998) *Margaret McMillan: 'I Learn to Succour the Helpless'.* Nottingham: Educational Heretics Press.

Mortimore, P. (2007) 'Will Academies take the easy option?' *Education Guardian,* Tuesday, November 6, p. 4.

Moss, P. (2003) 'Getting beyond childcare: reflections on recent policy and future possibilities', in J. Brannen and P. Moss (eds) *Rethinking Children's Care.* Buckingham: Open University Press, pp. 25–43.

Mossberger, K., Tolbert, C. and Stansbury, M. (2003) *Virtual Inequity: Beyond the Digital Divide.* Washington, DC: Georgetown University Press.

National Union of Teachers (2008) *In Good Faith: The Report of the Executive's Task Group on Faith Schools.* London: National Union of Teachers.

Neal, L. (2000) *Victorian Babylon: People, Streets, and Images in Nineteenth-century London.* New Haven, CT: Yale University Press.

Neeson, J. M. (1993) *Commoners: Common Right, Enclosure and Social Change in England, 1700–1820.* Cambridge, New York: Cambridge University Press.

Nicholson, S., Jordan, E., Cooper, J. and Mason, J. (2008) *Childcare and Early Years Providers Survey 2007.* British Market Research Bureau: DCSF.

Nickell, S. (2004) 'Poverty and worklessness in Britain', *The Economic Journal 114,* March, C1–C25.

Nie, N. and Erdring, L. (2000) 'Our Shrinking Social Universe', *Public Perspective,* 11 (3): 44–5.

Noble, D. (2002) *Digital Diploma Mills: The Automation of Higher Education.* New York Monthly Review Press.

Nunes, M. (2006) *Cyberspaces of Everyday Life*. Minneapolis, MN: University of Minnesota Press.

O'Connell Rust, F. (2003) 'Counting the cost of caring; intended and unintended consequences of early childhood policies', in J. P. Isenberg and M. J. Jalongo (2nd edn.) *Major Trends and Issues in Early Childhood Education. Challenges, Controversies and Insights*. 2nd edn. New York and London: Teachers College, Columbia University, pp. 153–63.

Odone, C. (2008) *In Bad Faith: The New Betrayal of Faith Schools*. London: Centre for Policy Studies.

ONS (Office for National Statistics) (2005) *Focus on Social Inequalities: 2005 Edition*. London: TSO.

Olssen, M., Codd, J. and O'Neill, A. M. (2004) *Education Policy. Globalization, Citizenship and Democracy*. London: Sage.

O'Malley, B. (1997) 'Educate to Liberate'. *Times Educational Supplement*. pp. 4–5, 27 June, London.

One Laptop Per Child (OLPC) (2008) *Vision: Children in the Developing World are Inadequately Educated*. Online. Available at: <http: //www-static.laptop.org/vision/index.shtml > (accessed 30 September 2009).

Oppenheim, C. (2009) *Don't Neglect Child Poverty: It Seems Labour Have Given up on Halving Child Poverty by 2010*. Online. Available at: <http://www.guardian.co.uk/commentisfree/2009/may/08/child-poverty> (accessed 10 May 2009).

Oppenheimer, T. (1997) *The Computer Delusion*. Online. Available at: <http://www.theatlantic.com/issues/97jul/computer.htm> (accessed 30 September 2009).

Orwell, G. (1949) *Nineteen Eighty-Four*. London: Secker and Warburg.

Organisation for Economic Co-operation and Development (OECD) (2001), *Employment Outlook*. Paris: OECD.

Osborne, J. (2006), 'Deconstructing professionalism in the early years: resisting the regulatory gaze', *Contemporary Issues in Early Childhood*, 7 (1): 5–14.

Osler, A. (2007) *Faith Schools and Community Cohesion: Observations on Community Consultations. A Runnymede Trust Interim Report*. London: The Runnymede Trust.

Osler, A. and Vincent, K. (2003) *Girls and Exclusion*. London: Routledge Falmer.

Ousley, Sir H. (2001) *Community Pride not Prejudice: Making Diversity Work in Bradford* (The Ousley Report). Bradford: Bradford Council.

Ozga, J. (2000) *Policy Research in Educational Settings. Contested Terrain*. Buckingham: Open University Press.

Pahl, R. (ed.) (1968) *Readings in Urban Sociology*. London: Pergamon.

Palloff, R. and Pratt, K. (1999) *Building Learning Communities in Cyberspace*. San Francisco, CA: Jossey-Bass.

Palmer, S. (2007) *Toxic Childhood: How the Modern World Is Damaging Our Children and What We Can Do about It*. London: Orion.

Park, R., Burgess, E. and McKenzie, R. (eds) (1925) *The City*. Chicago, IL: University of Chicago Press.

Parker-Jenkins, M., Hartas, D. and Irving, B. A. (2005) *In Good Faith. Schools, Religion and Public Funding*. Aldershot: Ashgate.

Parliamentary Health Committee (2008) *Health Inequalities*. Online. Available at: <http://www.publications.parliament.uk/pa/cm200809/cmselect/cmhealth/286/28608.htm> (accessed 25 July 2009).

Pearson, I. (2004) *The Network Society: Technology and Society. Learning Space.* Online. Available at: <http://openlearn.open.ac.uk/mod/resource/view.php?id=210527> (accessed 18 June 2009).

Peltzman, B. R. (1998) *Pioneers of Early Childhood Education.* Westport, CT: Greenwood Press.

Piachaud, D. and Sutherland, H. (2002) 'Child poverty', in J. Hills, J. Le Grand and D. Piachaud (eds) *Understanding Social Exclusion.* Oxford: Oxford University Press, pp. 141–54.

Pile, S. (2005) *Real Cities, Modernity, Space and the Phantasmagorias of City Life.* London: Sage.

Porfilo, B. and Malott, C. (eds) (2008) *The Destructive Path of Neoliberalism: An International Examination of Urban Education.* Rotterdam: Sense.

Porter, C. (2004) 'A typology of virtual communities: a multi-disciplinary foundation for future research', in *JCMC* Article 3, November 16, 10 (1): 1–24, Online. Available at: <http://jcmc.indiana.edu/vol110/issue1/porter.html> (accessed July 2007).

Prakash, G. and Kruse, K. M. (eds) (2008) *The Spaces of the Modern City: Imaginaries, Politics, and Everyday Life.* Princeton, NJ: Princeton University Press.

Pring, R. (2005) 'Faith schools: can they be justified?' in R. Gardner, J. Cairns and D. Lawton (eds) *Faith Schools: Consensus or Conflict?* London: Routledge Falmer, pp. 51–60.

Purnell, J. (2005) 'E-Learning and Virtual Schools: Giving Students and Teachers an Edge', *School Executive*, September/October, pp. 28–9.

Puttnam, D. (2008) 'Foreword, in *Transforming Schools for the Future?*, A collection of provocation papers.* Weybridge: Toshiba Information Systems, pp. 2–3.

Raban, J. (1974) *Soft City.* London: Hamish Hamilton.

Raffo, C. (2009) 'Interrogating poverty, social exclusion and New labour's programme of priority educational policies in England', *Critical Studies in Education*, 50 (1): 65–78.

Raphael Reed, L. (1995) 'Reconceptualising equal opportunities in the 1990s: a study of radical teacher culture in transition', in M. Griffiths and B. Troyna (eds) *Antiracism, Culture and Social Justice in Education.* Stoke-on-Trent: Trentham Books, pp. 77–96.

Reay, D. (1998) *Class Works.* London, UCL Press.

Reay, D. (2001) 'The paradox of contemporary femininities in education: combining fluidity with fixity', in B. Francis and C. Skelton (eds) *Investigating Gender.* Buckingham: Open University Press, pp. 152–63.

Reay, D. (2006) 'The zombie stalking English schools: social class and educational inequality', *British Journal of Educational Studies*, 54 (3): 288–307.

Reich, R. (1997) 'Why the rich are getting richer and the poor, poorer', in A. Halsey, H. Lauder, P. Brown and A. Wells (eds) *Education: Culture, Economy, Society.* Oxford: Oxford University Press, pp. 163–71.

Reid, I. and Brain, K. (2003) 'Education action zones: mission impossible?' *International Studies in the Sociology of Education*, 13 (2): 195–214.

Riley, K. (2008) 'Can schools successfully meet their educational aims without the clear support of their local communities?' in *Journal of Educational Change*, September, 9 (3): 311–16.

Rizvi, F. and Lingard, B. (2000) 'Globalisation and education: complexities and contingencies', *Education Theory*, 50 (4): 419–26.

Robertson, R. (1995) 'Glocalization: time-space and homogeneity-heterogeneity', in M. Featherstone, S. Lash and R. Robertson (eds) *Global Modernities*. London: Sage Publications, pp. 25–44.

Rousham, L. (1995) 'CAN calculators make a difference?' in J. Anghilieri (ed.) *Children's Mathematical Thinking in the Primary Years*. London: Cassell, 92–109.

Rutter, J. (1998) 'Refugee supplementary schools', *Language Issues*, 10 (1): 7–11.

Safia-Mirza, H. and Reay, D. (2000) 'Spaces and places of Black educational desire: rethinking Black supplementary schools as a new social movement', *Sociology*, 34 (3): 521–44.

Sanderson, M. (1983) *Education, Economic Change and Society in England 1780–1870*. London: The Macmillan Press.

Sassen, S. (1991) *The Global City*. Princeton, NJ: Princeton University Press.

Sassen, S. (1994, 2006 3rd edn.) *Cities in a World Economy*. Thousand Oaks, CA: Pine Forge Press.

Sassen, S. (2006) *Territory, Authority, Rights. From Medieval to Global Assemblages*. Princeton, NJ: Princeton University Press.

Saunders, P. (1981) *Social Theory and the Urban Question*. London: Hutchinson.

Saunders, P. (1986) 'Comment on Dunleavy and Pretceille', Society and Space *(Environmental Planning D)*, no. 4, pp. 153–63.

Savage, M. and Warde, A. (1993) *Urban Sociology, Capitalism and Modernity*. London: Macmillan.

Schon, D. (1973) *Beyond the stable State: Public and Private Learning in a Changing Society*. Harmondsworth: Penguin.

Selun, B. (2009) Personal correspondence (30 April 2009).

Selwyn, N. (1999) 'Why the computer is not dominating schools: a failure of policy or a failure of practice?' *Cambridge Journal of Education*, 29 (1): 77–91.

Sen, A. (1997) 'Human capital and human capability', *World Development*, 25 (12): 1959–61.

Sennett, R. (1990) *The Conscience of the Eye*. New York: Alfred A. Knopf.

Serra, A. (2000) 'Next generation community networking: futures for digital cities', in T. Ishida and K. Isbister (eds) *Digital Cities*. Berlin: Springer, pp. 45–57.

Shaw, W. (1997) 'Urban confidential: the "lurid" city of the 1950s', in D. B. Clarke (ed.) *The Cinematic City*. London and New York: Routledge, pp. 110–28.

Shell, B. (ed.) (1995) 'Shaping cyberspace into human space', *CSS Update* 6(3). Online. Available at: <http://fas.sfu.ca/css/update/vol6/6.3-harasim.main.html.> (accessed 4 December 2009).

Sheller, M. and Urry, J. (2006) 'Introduction: mobile cities, urban mobilities', in M. Sheller and J. Urry (eds) *Mobile Technologies of the City*. London: Routledge, pp. 1–17.

Shepherd, J. (2007) 'It's a world of possibilities', *The Guardian*, 8 May, p. 10.

Shiel, M. and Fitzmaurice, T. (eds) (2001) *Cinema and the City: Film and Urban Societies in a Global Context*. Oxford: Blackwell.

Shor, I. (1992) *Empowering Education: Critical Teaching for Social Change*. Chicago, IL: University of Chicago Press.

Silver, H. (1983) *Education as History: Interpreting Nineteenth- and Twentieth-Century History*. London: Methuen.

Simon, B. (1965) *Education and the Labour Movement 1870–1920*. London: Lawrence and Wishart.

Simon, B. (1974) *Education and the Labour Movement 1870–1920*. London: Lawrence and Wishart.

Simpson, O. (2005) 'E-learning, democracy, and social exclusion: issues of access and retention in the United Kingdom', in A. Carr-Chellman (ed.) *Global Perspectives on E-learning: Rhetoric and Reality*. London: Sage, pp. 89–100.

Sinfield, S. Holley, D. and Burns, T. (2009) A journey into silence: students, stakeholders and the impact of a strategic governmental policy document in the UK, in *Social Responsibility Journal*, Vol 5, No 4, Emerald Group Publishing Limited, pp. 566–574.

Skeggs, B. (1997) *Formations of Class and Gender*. London: Sage.

Skelton, T. and Valentine, G. (1998) *Cool Places: Geographies of Youth Cultures*. London and New York: Routledge.

Slater, J. (2006) 'The individual versus the collective in a time of globalisation: educational implications', in J. Kincheloe, K. Hayes, K. Rose and P. Anderson (eds) *The Praeger Handbook of Urban Education Volume 2*. Westport, CT: Greenwood Press, pp. 377–86.

Smidt, S. (2009) *Key Issues in Early Years Education: A Guide for Students and Practitioners*. 2nd edn. London: Routledge.

Smith, C. (2009) Augmented Reality. Personal correspondence (27 July 2009).

Smith, M. (2001) *Transnational Urbanism: Locating Globalisation*. Oxford: Blackwell.

Smith, F., Hardman, F. and Higgins, S. (2006) 'The impact of interactive whiteboards on teacher-pupil interaction in the National Literacy and Numeracy Strategies', *BERJ*, 32 (3): 443–57.

Social Trends, (2006) 'Household Internet Connection: by type', *National Statistics*. Online. Available at: <*www.statistics.gov.uk/socialtrends36/*> (accessed 7 April 2009).

Sparkes, J. and Glennerster, H. (2002) 'Preventing social exclusion: education's contribution', in J. Hills, J. Le Grand, D. Piachaud (eds) *Understanding Social Exclusion*. Oxford: Oxford University Press, pp. 178–201.

Spybey, T. (2001) 'The constitution of global society', in C. Bryant and D. Jary (eds) *The Contemporary Giddens: Social Theory in a Globalizing Age*. Basingstoke: Palgrave, pp. 147–67.

Squire, K. and Barab, S. (2004) Replaying History: Engaging Urban Underserved Students in Learning World History Through Computer Simulation Games. *Proceedings of the 6th International Conference on Learning Sciences*. California: Santa Monica.

Standage, T. (1999) *The Victorian Internet*. London: Phoenix.

Stedman-Jones, G. (1971) *Outcast London: A Study in the Relationship between Classes in Victorian Society*. Oxford: Clarendon Press.

Stedman-Jones, G (1992) *Outcast London: A Study in the Relationship between Classes in Victorian Society*. London: Penguin Books.

Stedman-Jones, G. (2004) *An End to Poverty?* London: Profile.

Stevenson, D. (2003) *Cities and Urban Cultures*. Maidenhead, Philadelphia: Open University Press.

Stone, M. (1985) *The Education of the Black Child: The Myth of Multiracial Education*. London: Fontana.

Stovall, D. (2006) Urban poetics: poetry, social justice and critical pedagogy in education. *The Urban Review*, March, 38 (1): 63–80.

Strand, S. (2007) 'Surveying the views of pupils attending supplementary schools in England', *Educational Research*, 49 (1): 1–19.

Strategy Unit (2005) *Connecting the UK: The Digital Strategy, a Joint Report with Department of Trade and Industry*. Crown: London.

Stromquist, N. and Monkman, K. (eds) (2000) *Globalization and Education: Integration and Contestation across Cultures*. Lanham, MD: Rowman and Littlefield.

Sullivan, J. (2000) *Catholic Schools in Contention: Competing Metaphors and Leadership Implications*. Dublin: Veritas.

SustainIT (2006) *ICT Case Study: Lambeth Link-Up Project*. Online. Available at: <http://www.sustainit.org/case-studies/docs/142-LambethLink.pdf > (accessed 22 July 2009).

Sutherland, G. (1971) *Elementary Education in the Nineteenth Century*. London: The Historical Association.

Swick, K. J. (2003) 'Working with families of young children', in J. P. Isenberg and M. J. Jalongo, *Major Trends and Issues in Early Childhood Education. Challenges, Controversies and Insights*. 2nd edn. New York and London: Teachers College, Columbia University, pp. 69–80.

Taylor, M. (2006) 'It's official: class matters', *The Education Guardian*. P.1. 28 February, London.

Taylor, M. and Evans, R. (2006) 'Sponsors fail to hand over academy cash', *The Guardian*, May, 3:1.

Te Riele, K. (ed.) (2009) *Making Schools Different: Alternative Approaches to Educating Young People*. London, New York: Sage.

Tettegah, S. (2005) 'Urban education and technology in the digital age', *Urban Education*, 40 (4): 363–7.

Thomson, J. (1870–1874) *The City of Dreadful Night*. Online. Available at: <www.cardiff.ac.uk/encap/skilton/poetry/thoms01a.html> (accessed 22 February 2008).

Thornton, L. and Brunton, P. (2009) *Understanding the Reggio Approach: Early Years Education in Practice*. London: David Fulton.

Thrasher, F. (1927) *The Gang*. Chicago, IL: University of Chicago Press.

Thrift, N. (2000) 'Not a straight line but a curve, or, Cities are not mirrors of modernity', in D. Bell and A. Haddow (eds) *City Visions*. Harlow: Pearson, pp. 233–63.

Thrupp, M. (2005) *School Improvement: An Unofficial Approach*. London: Continuum.

Thrupp, M. (2007) *Education's 'Inconvenient Truth': Persistent Middle Class Advantage*. An inaugural professorial lecture given at the University of Waikato, 2 March 2007.

Thrupp, M. and Tomlinson, S. (2005) Education policy, social justice and 'complex hope', *British Educational Research Journal*, 31 (5): 549–56

Tiffin, J. and Rajasingham, L. (1995) *In Search of the Virtual Class: Education in an Information Society*. London: Routledge.

Timmins, N. (1996) *Five Giants: A Biography of the Welfare State*. London: Fontana.

Tomlinson, S. (2005) *Education in a Post-Welfare Society*. 2nd edn. Maidenhead: Open University Press, McGrawHill.

Tomlinson, S. (2008) *Race and Education. Policy and Politics in Britain*. Maidenhead: McGraw-Hill Education.

Toshiba/Futurelab (2008) *Transforming Schools for the Future?* A collection of provocation papers. Weybridge: Toshiba Information Systems.

Toynbee, P. (2001) 'Religion must be removed from all functions of state', *The Guardian*, 12 December 2001.

Toynbee, P. (2003) *Hard Work: Life in Low Pay Britain.* London: Bloomsbury.

Toynbee, P. (2006) 'The fight against poverty is half-won. Now we need a radical plan', *The Guardian*, 10 March. Online. Available at: <http://www.guardian.co.uk/society/2006/mar/10/politics.homeaffairs> (accessed 14 May 2006).

Toynbee, P. and Walker, D. (2005) *Better or Worse? Has Labour Delivered?.* London: Bloomsbury Publishing.

Toynbee, P. and Walker, D. (2008) *Unjust Rewards. Exposing Greed and Inequality in Britain Today.* London: Granta.

Turkle, S. (1997) *Life on the Screen: Identity in the Age of the Internet.* London: Phoenix.

United Nations (2007) *World Urbanization Prospects: The 2007 Revision.* Online. Available at: <http://www.un.org/esa/population/publications/wup2007/2007wup.htm> (accessed 27 July 2009).

Valins, O. (2003) 'Defending identities or segregating communities? Faith-based schooling and the UK Jewish community', *Geoforum*, 34: 235–47.

Van Dijk, J. (1991) De Netwerkmaatschappij (translated in 1999, 2nd edn 2005) *The Network Society: Social Aspects of New Media* (original Dutch edition 1991). London: Sage.

Van Vliet, W. (2002) 'Cities in a globalizing world: from engines of growth to agents of change', *Environment and Urbanization*, April, 14 (1): 31–40.

Wacquant, L. (2007) *Urban Outcasts. A Comparative Sociology of Advanced Marginality.* Cambridge: Polity Press.

Walker, A. and Walker, C. (eds) (1997) *Britain Divided. The Growth of Social Exclusion in the 1980s and 1990s.* London: Child Poverty Action Group.

Walkerdine, V. (1992) 'Progressive pedagogy and political struggle', in C. Luke and J. Gore (eds), *Feminisms and Critical Pedagogy.* New York: Routledge, pp. 15–24.

Walkerdine, V. and Lucey, H. (1989), *Democracy in the Kitchen: Regulating Mothers and Socialising Daughters.* London: Virago Press.

Walkerdine, V. Lucey, H. and Melody, J. (2001) *Growing Up Girl.* Basingstoke: Palgrave.

Ward, H. (2008) Verdict: 'Not so Sure Start', *Times Educational Supplement*, October, pp. 10–31.

Watson, S. (1988) *Accommodating Inequality: Gender and Housing.* Sydney: Allen and Unwin.

Weller, P. (2006) 'Addressing religious discrimination and Islamophobia: Muslims and Liberal Democracies. The case of the United Kingdom', *Journal of Islamic Studies*, 17 (3): 295–325.

Wellman, B. (ed.) (1999) *Networks in the Global Village.* Boulder, CO: Westview.

Wellman, B. (2001) 'Physical place and cyberplace: the rise of personalized networking', *International Journal of Urban and Regional Research*, 25 (2): 227–52.

West, A., Pennell, H. and Hind, A. (2007) *Faith Schools – Selection by the Back Door?* Education Research Group, Department of Social Policy. London: London School of Economics. Online. Available at: <http://www.lse.ac.uk/collections/pressAndInformationOffice/newsAndEvents//archives/2007/FaithSchools.htm> (accessed 28 April 2009).

West, A., Xavier, R. and Hind, A. (2003) *Evaluation of Excellence Challenge by Extending and Adding to the Existing Evaluation of Excellence in Cities*. London: Department for Education and Skills.

Westwood, S. and Williams, J. (1996) (eds) *Imagining Cities: Scripts, Signs and Memory*. London: Routledge.

Whitty, G. (2002) *Making Sense of Education Policy*. London: Paul Chapman.

Whitty, G. (2008) 'Twenty Years of Progress? English Education Policy 1988 to the Present', *Educational Management Administration & Leadership*, 36 (2): 165–84.

Wiese, A. (2005) *Places of Their Own: African American Suburbanization in the Twentieth Century Chicago*. Chicago, IL: University of Chicago Press.

Wilkinson, R. and Pickett, K. (2009) *The Spirit Level: Why More Equal Societies Almost Always Do Better*. London: Allen Lane.

Williams, R. (1961) *The Long Revolution*. London: Chatto and Windus.

Williams, R. (1973) *The Long Revolution*. London: Penguin.

Williams, R. (2000) 'Metropolitan perceptions and modernism', in M. Miles and T. Hall with I. Borden (eds) *The City Cultures Reader*. 2nd edn. London and New York: Routledge, pp. 58–65.

Willis, P. (2006) 'Foot soldiers of modernity: the dialectics of cultural consumption and the twenty-first century school', in H. Lauder, P. Brown, J. Dillabough and A. Halsey (eds) *Education, Globalisation and Social Change*. Oxford: Oxford University Press, pp. 506–23.

Wilson, W. J. (1991) 'Studying inner-city social dislocation: the challenge of public agenda research', *American Sociological Review*, 56: 1–14.

Wilson, W. J. (1996) *When Work Disappears: The World of the New Urban Poor*. New York: Alfred A. Knopf.

Wilson, W. J. (1997) 'Studying inner-city social dislocations: the challenge of public agenda research', in A. Halsey, H. Lauder, P. Brown and A. Wells (eds) *Education: Culture, Economy, Society*. Oxford: Oxford University Press, pp. 750–64.

Wirth, L. (1928) *The Ghetto*. Chicago, IL: University of Chicago Press.

Wood, P. and Landry, C. (2007) *The Intercultural City: Planning for Diversity Advantage*. London and Sterling, VA: Earthscan.

Wright, C. (1992) *Race Relations in Primary Schools*. London: David Fulton.

Wrigley, T. (2006) *Another School Is Possible*. London: Bookmarks.

Zukin, S. (2003) 'Whose culture? Whose city?' in R. T. LeGates and F. Stout (eds) *The City Reader*. 3rd edn. London: Routledge, pp. 136–46.

Subject Index

Author Index